Sanctification in Reverse
The Essence of Satanic Ritual Abuse

By Patricia Baird Clark

Sanctification in Reverse
The Essence of Satanic Ritual Abuse
by Patricia Baird Clark

Copyright ©2013 Patricia Baird Clark

ISBN 978-1-935018-80-3

Patricia Baird Clark may be contacted through her website
at: www.hispresenceonline.org.

The King James Bible was used for scripture references.

Dedication

To my husband, Stoner, a learned man of God thoroughly acquainted with the Scriptures whose godly covering has protected me and allowed me freedom to explore the depths of God.

Table of Contents

PREFACE

This book is about good and evil...the greatest good and the greatest evil...both coming to fruition at the same time in the great end time harvest. These opposites, in type seen as two rivers, consist of people coming into the fullness of salvation in the Lord Jesus Christ, while at the same time others, many of whom are perpetrators of satanic ritual abuse, are coming into the fullness of evil.

It may seem strange to see these opposites presented in the same book, but because they exist concurrently, each affects the other. Confronting the fullness of evil head-on causes us to draw closer to God and grow stronger in faith and power. At the same time, there are many innocent people held captive by this heinous evil who need help from those who have the love and power of the Lord to set them free.

It is common knowledge that abuse is a fact of our times, but many people know nothing about a strange kind of abuse known as satanic ritual abuse. Satanic ritual abuse (SRA) is the practice of abusing an innocent person for the purpose of gaining satanic powers. The person is chosen for this purpose while an infant or small child. Some are even chosen from their mother's womb. The abuse continues throughout their lifetime and will only be stopped through the intervention of the Lord Himself. Most often God will use a yielded Christian vessel through whom He can set these prisoners free. Those who are willing to minister to these most wounded of all persons will find themselves growing closer to the Lord and learning many things about the kingdom of darkness and the awesome power of the kingdom of God.

Because much of this abuse is generational, cultists will often choose a child in their own family to be abused. Additionally other children may be used because they are available. When mom and dad are busy with other interests and children are left with caretakers, they are vulnerable. This often happens because people are ignorant of the existence and prevalence of this kind of abuse.

Satanic ritual abuse is abuse without limits…whatever an evil mind fueled by demons from hell can conjure up will be done to innocent children and the abuse will usually continue throughout their entire lifetime. They may be starved, buried alive, put in boxes or holes filled with snakes or spiders, repeatedly raped, forced to eat human flesh and drink blood, urinated and defecated on, denied sleep, beaten, burned, sold for sexual use, used in pornography, denied love or touch, have objects inserted in their body openings…the list is endless. Because the abuse is so horrendous and its effects so devastating, God's power and presence are available to them in abundance when a fellow Christian is willing to pray with them and bring them through the hell of their memories into wholeness. In the process of helping these desperately wounded people, the Christian helper will find God's grace, power and love coming into their own life in ways that are beyond what we could ever imagine. As we confront the kingdom of darkness, God brings us up into the kingdom of God.

Cultists have power to blind people's eyes so signs of abuse will not be recognized. In addition to this, people don't want to believe it. The typical response when told about this abuse is unbelief. Persons involved in the abuse are often trusted and respected members of society such as doctors, policemen, educators, government officials, etc. The abused person most often does not remember the abuse because of dissociation. They have also been threatened and intimidated not to tell.

Dissociation is a split in the conscious process in which a group of mental activities breaks away from the main stream of consciousness and functions as a separate unit, as if belonging to another person. It is a defense mechanism that enables a person to survive extreme trauma and often not remember it. It was once called "multiple personality disorder," but the term used now is "dissociative identity disorder."

Survivors of satanic ritual abuse usually cannot escape because they have been programmed for abuse. Cults through torture, hypnosis and sophisticated programming techniques cause them to form an abuse identity that locks them into the abuse. In addition to this, dissociated parts of themselves that are trained for the cult's use are in the unconscious mind where the conscious mind cannot access them. These parts work against the person. For this reason they need a prayer helper who can bring the presence of Jesus Christ to them. He, the King of kings and Lord of lords, will find these wounded parts and draw them unto Himself. The ministry experience not only brings healing to the abused person, but also both the abused person and the helper will see the kingdom of God opening to them in ways they otherwise would never have seen.

There is no way to determine how many persons have suffered such abuse because it is seldom reported and most who have been so abused do not remember it. They suffer the effects of the abuse but do not remember it because of dissociation. However, when one understands the purpose of the abuse, that satanic power comes from abusing the "living sacrifice," one can then determine that the abuse must be extremely common.

There have been concerns about "false memory syndrome," but when memories occur as an abreaction with demonic entities manifesting and speaking out of the person, there can be no doubt as to the fact of severe abuse. In an abreaction, the person is reliving the experience in every possible dimension and in great detail. They experience the emotions—they may scream, try to run away, vomit, etc. because of the intense horror of their experience. Also body memory is evident. For example a person having a memory of being beaten may have bruises appear on their body during the abreaction that coincide with the memory. To witness someone going through memories of this magnitude totally nullifies any doubts that they were horribly abused. This is far beyond someone making suggestions that could cause false memories.

When a Christian helper witnesses an abreaction along with demonic manifestations, he/she is seeing into the depths of a human soul and witnessing its interaction with the spirit world. Through prayer the Holy Spirit and sometimes angels are brought in to minister to the person. Demons are cast out by the helper in the power of God using the Sword of the Spirit. All this lifts the helper and the abused person up out of the natural, physical realm into the realm of the kingdom of God. It opens their eyes to see beneath the surface of all human interactions and strengthens their faith in God and His Word. This is definitely ministry that helps prepare us to enter the kingdom of God in these end times. Satan's attempts to bring in his evil kingdom actually backfire and the opposite occurs as those who confront him are actually lifted up into God's kingdom. Putting it another way, sanctification is enabled when the Devil's attempts to thwart it are discovered and God's intervention is brought in through prayer.

When satanic ritual abuse is seen as the exact antithesis of sanctification, it should become evident to the most adamant doubter that this abuse actually takes place. Seeing this abuse as sanctification in reverse will remove much of the mystery regarding why abusers do what they do to innocent victims. It is my prayer that this book will open the eyes of many to end time truths and spiritual realities... understandings we will need for the difficult days ahead.

INTRODUCTION

It is extremely difficult for people who have been satanically ritually abused to find persons who can minister to them effectively. God has heard their cries for deliverance and He is preparing a vast army of persons to minister to these people, an army that is presently sleeping. However, He is about to gently call to them, and they will awaken to find themselves successfully ministering to the most abused persons on the face of the earth—the satanically ritually abused.

This army is the Church. People abused in satanic cults have emotional problems that often cause them to seek help from mental health professionals. They frequently have labels placed on them such as schizophrenia, bipolar, borderline, psychotic, paranoid, etc. When we in the church hear these psychological terms, we automatically think we could never help such persons. However, this is far from the truth. The truth is the only person who can really set these persons free is Jesus, and we in the church have Jesus. He lives inside of us and is longing to be released to supernaturally minister to the abused. We must learn how to release Him so He can do this.

We have kept the Lord restrained behind our walls of fear and wrong beliefs. We live in a society that believes education and science hold the answers to our deepest problems, and we have agreed with them. Shame on us! I was the same way. When it was prophesied that I would minister to people who are the worst of the worst, psychologically speaking, I was flabbergasted. I didn't understand mental illness and I had no idea what to do. But the call persisted and soon God brought to me for help a severely abused woman suffering from DID, cult programming and multitudinous demons. All I knew to do was to learn a little about satanic ritual abuse (SRA) and then delve in and try. I was amazingly successful.

I believe I was successful because I didn't know what to do, but I had a relationship with Jesus. Out of that relationship, I learned to let Him lead. I wanted supernatural communication from the Lord—like visions, an audible voice, predetermined instructions, etc., but I received none of these. I had to just do whatever came into my mind—and wonder of wonders, it worked! My first abused woman had been labeled with many scary-sounding mental illnesses. She had been through several electric shock treatments. I knew I was in over my head—but that was a good thing. When I didn't know what to do, Jesus did.

My main purpose for committing myself to SRA ministry was to help the hurting. However, God had multiple purposes for calling me to this ministry. Yes, He wanted the prisoners set free, but also He had things He wanted to do in me. In my ignorance of what to do, I was learning to be more dependent upon Him which was drawing me deeper into relationship with Him. He was teaching me to listen to that still small voice within. He was filling me with His power as I encountered many powerful demons in the course of ministry. He wanted me to recognize evil in all its forms and see beneath the surface of society. All of these things and more were things God wanted to accomplish in me as I was setting others free by His power and love.

We in the church need to learn that ministry, first and foremost, flows out of a relationship with Jesus rather than education and techniques. The best preparation I can have to minister to severely abused persons is lots of time in the presence of the Lord, daily taking up my cross and allowing God to transform me into His image. Relationship is the key—relationship with Jesus and relationship with the abused person. This is far different than making an appointment with the professional to be seen once a week. This is not to denigrate the professionals who have totally given of themselves to help the abused—they have helped many and my hat goes off to them. I'm trying to awaken the Church to the fact that far more persons are needed and that we who have the Lord are equipped to minister. The most important prerequisite is that we be called to this ministry, and many are called who just don't know it yet!

God is calling us into His kingdom where things are done differently than the world does them. To say we don't need credentials and college degrees to minister to severely emotionally disturbed persons seems unbelievable, but think for a moment about Jesus. He had none of the world's credentials. He was a lowly carpenter. What He did have was a relationship with Father God, a relationship that enabled Him to say, "I only do what I see the Father do. I only say what I hear the Father say." He was totally dependent on His heavenly Father. We are to follow in His footsteps and become totally dependent on Jesus. This is a process and our ability to do this grows as we mature in Him.

Our belief in the need for special education has caused this vast army of ministers to be completely overlooked. Whenever I talk to someone who is a friend of an SRA person, they usually want me to minister to their friend or recommend some professional therapist. My response is often, "Why don't you minister to her. You are the one who has already gained her trust. You have the Holy Spirit. All you need is the call of God, a basic understanding of the principles behind SRA, a relationship with Jesus, and the willingness to spend time helping her."

Similarly, the first thing a person who feels called to SRA ministry thinks is, Where can I go to be educated in this so I can effectively minister? That was my response. I began working on a master's degree in counseling. After completing my first course, the Lord told me He wanted me to stop pursuing the degree. He led me to attend two or three short local seminars and then released me to minister.

Several years ago, after I had been ministering for satanic ritual abuse for about five years, I met a new friend who had attended many Christian seminars, had completed some college counseling courses and had a lot of knowledge. She showed me her notebook filled with instructions on how to minister. As I glanced through her notebook I thought, "On my! I don't know any of this stuff. Maybe I need to change the way I'm doing things." My friend suggested I take a few pages from her notebook and incorporate them in my ministry.

I tried this. I was ministering to an incredibly wounded lady who was absolutely shattered in her identity and we had been making remarkable progress. At our next session I announced I was going to try a different approach to ministry. We tried my new technique for awhile and she finally said, Can we please go back to doing things the way we were before? I readily agreed, and we got back on track. I was greatly relieved and so was she. What I had done was take control out of the hands of the Holy Spirit as I determined what we would do that day.

It is part of our nature to want to be in control. It is scary to enter into a ministry situation not knowing what to do. We have thoughts like, What if I fail? What will this person think of me? What if I don't really hear from God?

I'd like to give an illustration of a very successful ministry time that seemed to be going nowhere until I did something highly unusual. Everything I tried to do to help this lady was of no avail, and I was totally at a loss for how to help her. She had a problem in that her emotions were locked up and she was unable to release them. She had unconsciously stored all of her anger and rage (SRA persons are filled with rage) someplace deep inside, and it was just stuck there. She could feel it and knew it needed to come up but was powerless to do anything about it. I couldn't do anything either.

She was sitting there with a big pillow on her lap in case the anger came up and she needed to pound on something. We prayed and nothing happened, so we prayed some more and still nothing happened. We were sitting there and I had the thought, Sing "Break Forth into Joy." I thought, No, that's just me. The thought came again and I thought, That would be totally inappropriate. The thought persisted so I figured it must be the Lord. I opened my mouth and sang loudly, "Break forth into joy, O my soul. Break forth into Joy, O my soul, etc."

All of a sudden this lady jumped out of her chair and started yelling and cursing. She took the pillow and began pounding it with all her might, even kicking it. Then she was on her knees on the floor pounding the pillow. The foulest language I ever heard in my life was pouring out of her mouth as she yelled and screamed at her abusers until she was out of breath. Slowly she returned to herself and we could talk about what had just transpired. My obedience to sing loudly made her angry and that triggered the anger locked up within from abuse that occurred many years ago.

She had been afraid to express this anger and the foul language she knew would come out because she feared rejection from my husband and me (her pastors). This fear was fueled by things said to her by ministers from her past such as, "That kind of language is not acceptable. We don't talk like that around here."

My husband had heard the tirade and even peeked in my office door to make sure I was all right during the episode. As we walked out of my office, he gave her a hug and exclaimed, "Wow! You had a wonderful session in there." She was totally released from her fear of our rejection. We knew there was more rage buried down deep in her soul and when the time was right, more would be released. Hopefully the next time would be easier because of what had just happened. If I had not been obedient to do something that seemed very foolish, it probably wouldn't have happened.

What I did was risky. What if I sang like that and nothing happened? I would look like a fool. We have to be willing to appear foolish if we are to follow the Lord's leading. I wish I could hear His audible voice (like some of my abused friends can), but usually the

Lord just gives me a thought. What we need to understand is that the more we are conformed to His image in our daily walk with Him, the more our thoughts become His thoughts. Or perhaps I should say His thoughts become our thoughts. Either way, we are in process of becoming one with Jesus to the point that we think as He does.

Henri Nouwen, in his book, *In the Name of Jesus*, made a comment about leadership that would be good advice for anyone in ministry: "… leadership must be rooted in the permanent, intimate relationship with the incarnate Word, Jesus, and they need to find there the source for their words, advice, and guidance." (Nouwen 1989, 31)

This book, *Santification in Reverse*, is based on the first twelve verses of Ezekiel 47 where the course of a powerful healing river is described. Each verse will reveal certain aspects of sanctification believers will need to fulfill for entering into completion in Christ Jesus. After each point, an aspect of its antithesis as seen in satanic ritual abuse will be explained.

As the church proceeds further into the end of this age and the time of the harvest, we will witness the simultaneous ripening of the fullness of righteousness and the fullness of evil. Both are described in this unique revelation. Each, by itself, would be difficult to believe, but when viewed together, one lends credulity to the other.

Ministers and counselors all over the world are encountering the bizarre effects of satanic ritual abuse manifested in persons needing help that are beyond one's scope of information to process. The Bible seems strangely silent on many of these things, but in actuality it has much to say that is buried beneath the surface waiting to be uncovered by the saints of the end times. May this book be the catalyst to spark a renewed hunger in God's people for deep study of the Word of God where the answers to many mysteries are waiting to be uncovered.

EZEKIEL FORTY-SEVEN
Verses 1-12

1 Afterward he brought me again unto the door of the house; and, behold, waters issued out from under the threshold of the house eastward: for the forefront of the house stood toward the east, and the waters came down from under from the right side of the house, at the south side of the altar.

2 Then brought he me out of the way of the gate northward, and led me about the way without unto the utter gate by the way that looketh eastward; and, behold, there ran out waters on the right side.

3 And when the man that had the line in his hand went forth eastward, he measured a thousand cubits, and he brought me through the waters; the waters were to the ankles.

4 Again he measured a thousand, and brought me through the waters; the waters were to the knees. Again he measured a thousand, and brought me through; the waters were to the loins.

5 Afterward he measured a thousand; and it was a river that I could not pass over: for the waters were risen, waters to swim in, a river that could not be passed over.

6 And he said unto me, Son of man, hast thou seen this? Then he brought me, and caused me to return to the brink of the river.

7 Now when I had returned, behold, at the bank of the river were very many trees on the one side and on the other.

8 Then said he unto me, These waters issue out toward the east country, and go down into the desert, and go into the sea: which being brought forth into the sea, the waters shall be healed.

9 And it shall come to pass, that every thing that liveth, which moveth, whithersoever the rivers shall come, shall live: and there shall be a very great multitude of fish, because these waters shall come thither: for they shall be healed; and every thing shall live whither the river cometh.

10 And it shall come to pass, that the fishers shall stand upon it from Engedi even unto Eneglaim; they shall be a place to spread forth nets; their fish shall be according to their kinds, as the fish of the great sea, exceeding many.

11 But the miry places thereof and the marshes thereof shall not be healed; they shall be given to salt.

12 And by the river upon the bank thereof, on this side and on that side, shall grow all trees for meat, whose leaf shall not fade, neither shall the fruit thereof be consumed: it shall bring forth new fruit according to his months, because their waters they issued out of the sanctuary: and the fruit thereof shall be for meat, and the leaf thereof for medicine.

CHAPTER ONE

In January of 1996 my husband and I moved from Newark, Ohio to Rochester, New York in the midst of a major snow storm. The men of the church had helped us load the U-haul truck on Saturday, our final church service was Sunday, and Monday we were to leave for our new home in New York. However, nobody was going anywhere that Monday due to the storm. Even the Interstates were closed. So we slept on the floor that night hoping for better weather the next day.

As it turned out, the Interstates were open the next day in spite of the fact it was still snowing, and we made our trip, my husband driving the U-haul and me following behind in the van. It was a long trip and I did a lot of slipping and sliding in the van, but we made it to our new parsonage that night after a thirteen-hour drive which under better conditions would have taken seven hours.

Even though we arrived much later than anticipated, there were church people waiting for us at the parsonage to help unload the truck and set up our bed so we could sleep there that night. That was when I met a certain lady whom I came to discern in the weeks that followed as someone who was incredibly severely, satanically ritually abused.

I had decided before leaving Ohio that when we got to New York I wasn't going to say a word about the satanic ritual abuse ministry. It is a topic that can upset church-goers and run people out of your church quickly. We had learned this the hard way. However, every time this abused lady, who had no idea she was abused, came around me she started trembling and crying. I sensed God was working in her. She and her husband, who had attended that church for twenty years, were at the church every time the doors were open, so I saw a lot of her... and she did a lot of crying. I was concerned that others, who could complain about us to our overseers, were watching. The rejection I had experienced because of this ministry at our former church was fresh in my mind, and my plans to remain silent about it were obviously falling apart.

I knew the Lord was telling me to minister to her, so my first step was to develop more relationship with her. I took her to lunch. During our time together she started pouring out her heart to me, and we started meeting for ministry on a regular basis. Her satanic ritual abuse memories that were just below the surface of her conscious mind began coming up for the Lord's ministry.

Three months later we, and other women from our church, went to a women's conference in a nearby city. I roomed with my new friend. The first morning there we were both up early for prayer in our room. I was sitting at a desk with my back to her praying silently. She was sitting on the bed for her prayer time.

I had just silently asked God for a double portion of His Spirit when she spoke up saying, "I just had a vision. I saw Jesus come over to you and place two cloaks on you. One was red and the other was purple." That was the beginning of her ministry to me. It took seven years of meeting almost daily for her to complete her satanic ritual abuse memories, and after each session, the Lord gave her a word or a vision for me. His messages for me were always of love and encouragement.

About a year after I started ministering her, she had a vision where Jesus and I were married. I didn't really understand it but thought perhaps the Lord's message was that I was growing in maturity. After all, we, the Church of the end times are to be the bride of Christ.

Then a few days after that she had a vision where she saw Jesus and me sitting on a large flat rock in a beautiful meadow. We were just sitting there talking together when He reached down, touched my feet and said, "These feet will never touch the earth again." I had no idea what that was about either.

Shortly after going to bed that evening, I was lying in the dark all relaxed and waiting for sleep to come, when suddenly I felt a strange sensation in my feet. It was a very pleasant, rhythmic, tingling feeling quite unlike anything I had ever felt. The feeling quickly spread up my legs, over the trunk of my body and into my arms and hands. Immediately I thought about the vision of that day. The sensation had started in my feet. I knew it was Jesus and that I had been lifted up into a new spiritual dimension reserved for the Church of the end times. That was why He had said my feet would never touch the earth again. I also understood why she had had a vision of Jesus and me being married. This experience is the beginning of the second coming of Christ when the Bridegroom comes for His bride. Someone had to experience this early in order to be able to help others when their time comes for this experience. More about this later.

I would describe this new feeling as being a very gentle, slow rhythmic feeling almost like a deep massage but it doesn't touch the skin. It is deep inside and gives me the feeling of being deeply loved. Every fiber of my being feels loved. It is like bobbing up and down on a raft resting upon gentle waves like one would experience in a large lake or perhaps in a river. Ocean waves would be too strong. These are gentle waves. They never, ever stop...not for one second. My whole being feels this wonderful sense of God's love and quickening. It is deeply relaxing and comforting.

This wonderful feeling has remained with me and even intensified over the fifteen years since I had this experience. I know it will never stop because Jesus awakened my spiritual body that night. Once awakened, it will never again go back to its pre-awakened, dormant state. Also I remember clearly Jesus saying that my feet would never touch the earth again.

There is a spiritual side to our being that went dormant at the time of the fall when Adam and Eve were cast out of the garden. That was part of the death they experienced that came upon all humankind. This understanding explains what really happened when God said they would surely die on the day they sinned, and yet they lived for hundreds of years afterward in their human flesh. Part of them actually did die at the time of their sin. In these end times, God will be awakening this side of our being that is comprised of our spiritual body and our spiritual mind.

I believe God allowed me to experience this prior to others for two reasons: (1) He wanted someone to prepare books and teachings about it to give understanding to others when they have the experience. Since I study the Bible in depth every day using the study method Jesus revealed to me (see the last chapter of this book), I was one to whom He could reveal His deep secrets reserved for the Church of the end times. Only one who has had this experience could recognize it in Scripture. (2) At the same time I was also involved in the satanic ritual abuse (SRA) ministry. Satanic ritual abuse, in its most severe form, opens the veils in its victims to the spirit world in that their spiritual body and spiritual mind are awakened by demons so they can be terrorized by demons. When I minister to these people by inviting the Lord's presence to minister to them, the good spiritual realm can also be perceived by them such that they are able to see visions and hear words from the Lord. This is how my friend was able to have so many visions and words from God for me. The veil was open to her because of her severe abuse. Although she was not the only SRA person to have words for me, she definitely had the most.

I believe it is needful for someone who has been beyond the veil to help lead others through their veils into the supernatural realm reserved for the Church of the end times. Without my friend's many visions and words from God, I would not have understood what was happening to me. I used to wonder how others would understand their experience without someone like my friend to guide them. After years of study, writing books, and making YouTube videos I understand now that my teachings will help others through. Additionally, I pray others in the church will begin helping SRA persons so they can not only help others, but also have a similar experience of the opening of the supernatural as I had.

Concurrent with the words and visions from God, I was daily casting out very powerful demons from my friend. It was years of "new levels, new devils." As I grew in spiritual power according to the increasing presence of the Holy Spirit in my life, the demons I encountered in my friend became increasingly powerful. This is because Jesus was in charge, and He would only release demons that He knew I could handle. (This is described in detail in my book *Restoring Survivors of Satanic Ritual Abuse*).

To be open to the spiritual realm is to be open to both the evil and the good spiritual realms. When our heart is purified, a process that takes place as we are willing to allow the cross to lead us daily to our death to self, then we will not be deceived or troubled by demons. We see according to what is in our heart. That is why it is the pure in heart who shall see God. Any darkness in our heart blocks our view of Him and opens us up to demonic deception.

Another important thing about the SRA ministry is that it opens the minister's eyes to see strange, supernatural manifestations that most of us are not able to explain in our limited spiritual understanding and experience. If we are daily involved in Bible study, we will find the Holy Spirit showing us things in His Word that correspond to what we are seeing in ministry.

When I first started in the SRA ministry, a prophet told me that this ministry was preparation for another ministry God had for me. I didn't understand how this could be at the time. Now I see how the SRA ministry actually prepared me to understand the process we will all be going through as this mortal puts on immortality. Those to whom I ministered had experienced the evil awakening of their spiritual side. I was granted the privilege of having my spiritual side awakened by Jesus Christ. This awakening is still in progress.

It is almost unbelievable, but true, that the satanic ritual abuse ministry will serve to enlighten those who are willing to minister to these people such that these helpers will find themselves being gently drawn into the kingdom of God. The combination of ministry with Bible study opens our eyes to spiritual realities that were intended to be known only by the great Church of the end times.

With that said, I hope the reader will now see that the two rivers, the river of sanctification flowing out from God and the river of evil from the Devil, can best be understood when seen as opposites that run concurrently in these end times.

The Great River Journey

In Ezekiel 47 there is the account of a magnificent healing river that flows out from the temple of God. The trees on either side of this river are fruit-yielding trees whose leaves are for healing. The Holy Spirit wants us to join Him on a journey down this river, not in a boat, but immersed in the waters, for it is a river "to swim in." As we swim down the river we will see many trees, the east country, a desert, miry places, marshes, a multitude of fish, fishermen casting their nets and finally the sea. Each of these things we view will actually be spiritually interpreted as parts of ourselves, parts that need to be healed, awakened or removed if we are to come into the fullness of Christ.

Such a river never existed historically and, therefore, needs to be understood spiritually as explained in Adam Clarke's Commentary on the Old Testament:

> Literally, no such waters were ever in the temple; and because there were none, Solomon had what is called the brazen sea made, which held water for the use of the temple. It is true that the water which supplied this sea might have been brought by pipes to the place: but a fountain producing abundance of water was not there, and could not be there, on the top of such a hill; and consequently these waters, as well as those spoken

of in Joel 3:18, and in Zechariah 14:8, are to be understood spiritually or typically; and indeed the whole complexion of the place here shows, that they are thus to be understood. (Clarke 1966)

These waters have been understood down through the ages as having different spiritual connotations. For my spiritual interpretation, I am viewing this river as a representation of the gradual stages of growth in the life of a believer in the end times that culminates in the full salvation of the Lord Jesus Christ manifested in his/her life. This level of perfection has never been possible to anyone before this time. Jesus is coming for a bride without spot or wrinkle. Coming into this perfection...full sanctification...is a process that will be described here in our river journey.

It is only when we find healing and wholeness within our own being that Jesus Christ can manifest His life through us to a lost and dying world. Jesus said, "The kingdom of God is within you" (Luke 17:21). The western world, by and large, being caught up in materialism, has focused on outward things, but the kingdom of God is all about inward realities. "The kingdom of God is not meat and drink" (outward), "but righteousness, and peace, and joy in the Holy Ghost" (inward). The people of Jesus' day wanted Him to set up an earthly kingdom (outward) but Jesus said, "My kingdom is not of this world" (inward).

Sanctification

Since I am exposing satanic ritual abuse as being the reverse of sanctification, it would be good to briefly state what I mean by "sanctification." Guy Duffield and Nathaniel Van Cleave in *Foundations of Pentecostal Theology*, explain that there are three stages of sanctification. The first is positional in that the moment a person is born again, the holiness of Jesus is imputed to him. It is not yet being lived out in his daily life but has been put into "his account." The second aspect of sanctification is seen as a "continuing process throughout a Christian's entire lifetime…as we grow in grace and in the knowledge of our Lord and Savior Jesus Christ" (2 Pet. 3:18). The third aspect of sanctification will come at the time of the second coming of the Lord Jesus when we will reach sinless perfection and be wholly sanctified and awaiting his return…

> At that time we will be delivered "from the body of this flesh." "For our conversation is in heaven; from whence also we look for the Savior, the Lord Jesus Christ: who shall change our vile body, that it may be fashioned like unto his glorious body, according to the working whereby he is able to subdue all things unto himself" (Phil. 3:20, 21). "To the end he may establish your hearts unblameable in holiness before God, even our Father, at the coming of our Lord Jesus Christ with all his saints" (1 Thess. 3:13). We have been saved from the penalty of sin; we are being saved from the power of sin; we shall yet be saved from the presence of sin. "Beloved, now are we the sons of God, and it doth not yet appear what we shall be: but we know that, when he shall appear, we shall be like him; for we shall see him as he is" (1 John 3:2). In the meantime we are encouraged to "grow in grace, and in the knowledge of our Lord and Savior Jesus Christ" (2 Pet. 3:18). Beholding the glory of the Lord as in a glass, we are "changed into the same image from glory to glory, even as by the Spirit of the Lord" (2 Cor. 3:18). (Duffield and Van Cleave 1983)

The healing river will show us the third aspect of sanctification in detail as to how our entire being will be sanctified and changed into sinless perfection as we anticipate the Lord's appearing. Jesus triumphed over sin when He took the sins of the whole world upon Himself and died on the cross in our place. By believing in Him and receiving His eternal life, we too have died to sin. However, this is a positional reality that has to be walked out experientially in our lives. The sin principle is still alive in us at this present time as evidenced by the fact that sin, sickness and death are still part of our lives. The healing river will show that we will actually experience freedom from the sin principle and triumph experientially over the curse we inherited via Adam's fall.

As we examine each aspect of Ezekiel's healing river, we will see how Christ works in us to transform us into His image. We will also learn the reverse—how the Devil uses these principles and perverts them to turn people into empty shells devoid of humanness and then fills them with demon powers in preparation and anticipation of the rise of the Antichrist. Most specifically we will be examining in detail the perversion called satanic ritual abuse—what I believe to be the greatest evil of all time.

In his book, *People of the Lie*, Dr. M. Scott Peck reflects on what evil really means:

> It is a reflection of the enormous mystery of the subject that we do not have a generally accepted definition of evil. Yet in our hearts I think we all have some understanding of its nature. For the moment I can do no better than to heed my son, who, with the characteristic vision of eight-year-olds, explained simply, "Why, Daddy, evil is 'live' spelled backward." Evil is in opposition to life. It is that which opposes the life force. (Peck 1983, 42)

As we study the healing river, we will see the ultimate of life—people coming into the fullness of Christ, contrasted with the ultimate of evil in its wicked, backwards perversion—satanic ritual abuse.

The Reverse of Sanctification

Satanic Ritual Abuse consists of the bizarre twisting of the principles of sanctification into a form that is beyond recognition. Fiendish demons from hell have debased biblical truths into contorted, hellish perversions that don't even resemble the True. In Ezekiel's healing river, the plan for bringing humankind into the fullness of Christ will lead us straight into heaven itself. The river of the Devil flows into hell and many are those being swept away in its wake. The Healing River reveals the various stages God will take us through to be fully conformed to His image. Demons have taken this reality, turned it upside down into a counterfeit that has deceived humans and led them backwards into a wicked step-by-step method for coming into the fullness of evil.

Concerning counterfeits and reality, Glenn Clark, founder of Camps Farthest Out and author of more than 50 books, wrote an incredible explanation of the way Jesus looked at reality. Jesus saw everything in life as a parable—a parable being an allegorical relation of something real. What we would see as the cold, hard facts of life, Jesus looked through and used His imagination to see the eternal realities behind the facts. Our word "fact" comes from the word factum, meaning "something we do or make." We make quarrels, unhappiness, treachery, covetousness, etc. but these are not reality. Jesus looked beyond these things and concentrated on the reality that eternally is. Quarrels are made (fact), but love is (eternal reality). Unhappiness is made, but joy is. Lies are made, but truth is.

This is not to say Jesus was oblivious to the sin and brokenness in the lives around Him, but He was able to see something eternal and good in spite of the "facts." He could look straight through the facts of life knowing they were mere counterfeits or distorted reflections of an eternal reality. He was able to look at the dead little girl, see past the fact into the reality and utter this parable, "The girl is not dead, but sleeping" (Matt. 9:24).

This is the approach we need to take when confronted with the phenomenon of satanic ritual abuse. The horrible things done to people in the name of Satan are perversions of God's truth. The tremendous evil and the supernatural manifestations we encounter are merely counterfeits and twisted reflections of an eternal reality. The Devil cannot create anything. He can only take that which God has created and pervert it. Everything God has made is good. If we will take the approach Jesus took and look through the evil of SRA with parabolic eyes, we will begin to see the reality of which SRA is only a twisted reflection. By taking this approach, SRA will no longer be the baffling mystery it has seemed to be in the past. When we understand why things were done, we will be better equipped to help survivors out of their confusion and suffering.

The healing river's satanic counterfeit can be seen in Revelation 12:15 where "...the serpent cast out of his mouth water as a flood after the woman, that he might cause her to be carried away of the flood." The cults have gone further down this river of filth that flows from the serpent's mouth than the church has traveled down the river of healing and sanctification in that they experience more outward supernatural phenomena than the church.

The lives of true believers are being formed quietly, hidden away from the glare of public scrutiny much the same way the stones for Solomon's temple were formed. "And the house, when it was in building, was built of stone made ready before it was brought thither: so that there was neither hammer nor ax nor any tool of iron heard in the house, while it was in building" (1 Kings 6:7). The stones were prepared first underground and then brought forth completed to take their place in the temple.

There is nothing more supernatural than a transformed life. The death of our carnal nature and the life of Christ formed in us is the greatest miracle of all, but it doesn't attract the world's attention. The satanic cult supernatural is different in nature. They see and talk with demons, walk on hot coals without being burned, practice levitation, cast powerful spells on others and supposedly fly around in their spirit bodies (astral projection) thinking church folk to be weak fools. Little do they know they are totally deceived, living a counterfeit spirituality that will result in the loss of their own soul.

Satanists do not realize the fact that believers in these last days are going to follow God's plan for sanctification into the fullness of Christ and enter into power such as the world has never seen. The Devil has deceived Satanists into believing they can kill off 90% of the world's population and then take the remainder as their slaves. They do not see the Church as the sleeping giant that it is nor can they imagine the formidable power of Jesus Christ they will soon encounter head-on through the Church.

The Temple

In Ezekiel 47, the healing river is flowing out from the temple. We know that in the Old Testament there was a literal temple in Jerusalem that contained the Ark of the Covenant where God dwelt, but in the New Testament the focus changes from the literal temple (destroyed in 70 A.D.) to human beings as the temple of God. Immanuel (God with us) came to dwell in His people when He gave us His Holy Spirit.

In this study of Ezekiel's temple, we will be looking at an Old Testament account through New Testament eyes. All the descriptions of the temple are really descriptions of spiritual realities within the believer. The waters flowing out represent the Holy Spirit. We will see these waters flowing out of our spirit, into our soul and our body, bringing us to new levels of sacrifice and devotion to Jesus. We will see these spiritual waters activating the unused portion of our mind and awakening our spiritual body (unknown aspects of our being readily seen in satanic ritual abuse survivors), healing our bodies and opening the eyes of our heart enabling us to see, hear, feel and understand our Lord in ways humanity has never before experienced. In short, we see here in the account of these healing waters, the personal coming of the presence of Jesus Christ to a believer, working within to transition him/her from an earthbound, mortal existence into a supernatural, heavenly dimension reserved for those alive on earth in the last days of this closing age. This is a picture of a mortal putting on immortality (1 Cor. 15:53). These changes will enable us to enter fully into the coming age of miracles where we will do those greater works promised by Jesus in John 14:12.

I believe we are the generation who will face the events foretold by Jesus in Matthew 24 where He spoke of great tribulation and the need for the days to be shortened lest all humanity be destroyed. We will face great upheavals, judgment and transition. We will need to change from a temporal focus to a heavenly, spiritual focus. Should the delicate balance of our society suffer a breakdown, such as could be brought about by the fall of our economy, weapons of mass destruction or great natural disasters, many Christians will suddenly realize God is more important than anything in their lives. There will be a re-shifting of our priorities. Whereas God has been far down on the priority list of many Christians, these events should cause Him to become our very life or we will have no life. This study in Ezekiel reveals the coming of Jesus to the believer and the changes that He initiates in order to prepare us for the transition from this present age into the coming age of miracles.

Living Waters

Let us begin our exploration of this healing river with an in-depth look at the first verse of Ezekiel 47:

> *Afterward he brought me again unto the door of the house; and, behold, waters issued out from under the threshold of the house eastward: for the forefront of the house stood toward the east, and the waters came down from under from the right side of the house, at the south side of the altar. (Ezekiel; 47:1)*

These are the waters spoken of by Jesus in John 7:37, 38, "In the last day, that great day of the feast, Jesus stood and cried, saying, 'If any man thirst, let him come unto me, and drink. He that believeth on me, as the scripture hath said, out of his belly shall flow rivers of living water.'" In verse 39 John adds this explanation, "(But this spake he of the Spirit, which they that believe on him should receive: for the Holy Ghost was not yet given; because that Jesus was not yet glorified.)" This river in Ezekiel is none other than the Spirit of God flowing into the believer's spirit and from there going out into his entire being and then out to others.

It is significant that Jesus spoke these words at the Feast of Tabernacles because, as we shall see, the Feast of Tabernacles is, in type, referring to a great outpouring of the Spirit of God yet to come. It is true that these living waters have been flowing forth throughout the New Testament age, but it is only in these last days it becomes a mighty healing river that encompasses all parts of our being.

There were three feasts celebrated yearly by the Israelites at God's command: the Feast of Passover, the Feast of Pentecost and the Feast of Tabernacles. We know that the Feast of Passover, with the slaying of an unblemished lamb, was an Old Testament type of the New Testament reality of salvation. The Holy Spirit fell on the 120 persons in the upper room during the Feast of Pentecost (Acts 2), showing this Old Testament feast was a type of the baptism of the Holy Spirit. The last feast of the year, the Feast of Tabernacles, was the only time the high priest was allowed to enter into the Holy of Holies (in the tabernacle or temple) where the Spirit of God dwelt between the cherubim over the Ark of the Covenant. This happened on a certain day during the Feast of Tabernacles called the Day of Atonement.

The Feast of Tabernacles is an Old Testament type that is yet to be fulfilled—the Church coming into the manifest presence of Jesus Christ. We, as believers, are to enter into the Holy of Holies, into God's presence, in these last days. It is time for the Day of Atonement (at-one-ment), that we may become one with Christ as He manifests His fullness to us and in us.

These living waters flowing out from God will give an ever-deepening sense of His presence. Just as Christ is in us and we are in Him, the river is in us but also we are in the river. Our first glimpse of this river is in the Garden of Eden where, as it left the garden, it was divided into four separate rivers named Pison, Havilah, Gihon and Euphrates. These rivers have been understood according to some of the early Church Fathers as being four distinct ways we receive truth... through our own spiritual intuition, our natural senses, what is learned from the testimony of others, and our own deductions based on all we have learned from the aforementioned three. When the curse is lifted from us, we will once again be able to receive truth as it was in the Garden of Eden...in one flowing stream.

We see the river again in the last book of the Bible as "a pure river of water of life, clear as crystal, proceeding out of the throne of God and of the Lamb" (Rev. 22). We have a throne within us. Sometimes we are seated on that throne making our own decisions and living independently of God, but when we are mature and yielded to Christ, He will be seated upon that throne. Then there shall be no more curse and we shall see His face and His name shall be in our foreheads (Rev. 22:4).

The River of Evil

In stark contrast to the living water of the Lord Jesus, there is the filthy water that flows out of the mouth of the serpent. There are actually two rivers that bring people into a realm of spirit and supernatural power— one flows out from God and the other flows out from Satan. "And the serpent cast out of his mouth water as a flood after the woman, that he might cause her to be carried away of the flood" (Rev 12:15).

Unfortunately, Satan's river is flowing more freely in our society than God's through books (such as the Harry Potter books) and especially the electronic media. Think about what flows into our homes through TV, movies and music, and compare it with the following list of sins in Romans One where God gave them over to a reprobate mind because they were filled with "all unrighteousness, fornication, wickedness, covetousness, maliciousness; full of envy, murder, debate, deceit, malignity; whisperers, backbiters, haters of God, despiteful, proud, boasters, inventors of evil things, disobedient to parents, without understanding, covenant-breakers, without natural affection, implacable, and unmerciful." If that doesn't describe an evening of television, I don't know what does! And the next verse in Romans says "Who knowing the judgment of God, that they which commit such things are worthy of death, not only do the same, but have pleasure in them that do them." When we watch these things on television, we are having pleasure in them or we wouldn't be watching them. We need to examine ourselves to see exactly which river we are swimming in.

The satanically ritually abused are especially vulnerable to the evil coming over the television in that it can release demons within them or call to the surface of their mind wicked alternate personalities from their unconscious mind to fulfill their assignments. A famous person can deliver a speech before the nation and by using certain hand motions, trigger alternate personalities in the SRA to come forth. I have personally watched this happen to a woman in my own home. Certain movies aired on TV will have the same affect. I believe it is possible, through the use of codes, to trigger an entire nation of SRA persons as they watch particular programs they have been programmed to watch. We need to remember, though, that God is in control, and those SRA persons who have chosen Jesus Christ as their Savior will not be as vulnerable to these things as those who have not. God will only let the cults' plans go so far and then He will stop them. Everything, even Satanism, ultimately works out to further God's purpose in the earth as those things the wicked intended for evil, God ultimately works for good.

Satanists may have traveled further down their river than Christians have theirs in that they experience more supernatural phenomena; however, that will soon change. God has been working in the hearts of believers, transforming them into His image. Some of these more mature believers will be completing their journey down the healing river and the result will be a ministry coming forth such as the world has never seen.

At the same time believers are entering into the presence of God, Satanists are coming more into the presence of demons. God, being omnipresent, is everywhere at once, but Satan can only be in one place at a time. However, he has powerful demons—multitudes of them—that can be all over the world at one time. As Christians are becoming one with Christ, the Satanists are becoming one with demons to the point there is practically nothing human left in them. When one hears SRA memories, one sees how totally devoid of humanity Satanists become in their rituals. There is not one ounce of decency or compassion in them and there are no limitations to their acts of cruelty and perversion. They become animalistic and barbarous, devoid of all characteristics we think of as being human.

The Feast of Tabernacles took place in the fall at the time of the harvest. This present age, in which we are living, is also a time of great harvest when we will see not only the greatest good of all the ages come to fruition but also the fullness of evil manifested. The evil that has been hidden from our view and practiced only in dark, secret places is now coming blatantly out into the open for the whole world to see. The public has become "anesthetized" as the evil supernatural has been revealed a little at a time. Now that the evil supernatural is being attractively packaged through the Harry Potter books and movies, darkness is encompassing our entire nation.

Some may think I am overemphasizing the Potter books, but any spiritually sensitive person has to see the power behind the books. Children who never liked to read will now read books with 300 to 700 pages. That's power! But this power is not of God. The children are driven and obsessed with reading these books. It all looks so innocent, but the truth is, young, impressionable minds are being filled with the allure of witchcraft and the demonic. The ramifications of this upon the world have yet to be seen, but there is no doubt that young readers, hungering for more, will easily be led into deeper darkness, perhaps even to satanic rituals where they may be severely abused. A very young child can experience this kind of abuse and then lock it out of memory in the unconscious mind. The conscious memory of the abuse is not there, but the effect of what happened will dramatically affect their life and they will be enslaved to the darkness. Even if this worst scenario never happens, the love of witchcraft will certainly blind spiritual eyes to the truth of the Gospel and open their lives to demonic oppression and guidance.

Our society's love affair with Harry Potter's witchcraft and spells will not leave the Christians unaffected. By way of illustration I will share a true story. A friend of mine (relatively new to the faith, a sincere believer and faithful to our church) missed church one Sunday. I called her and left a message on her answering machine but she didn't return my call. A few days later she called to cancel our swimming engagement for that afternoon stating she didn't feel well. She had been in bed for days, depressed and not eating. I prayed with her on the phone in English and also in a prayer tongue.

The next day she called and told me what happened when I prayed in tongues with her. Her body began jerking on one side and when she hung up the phone, she felt better. She reached for her Bible and found that she was able to read it for the first time in days. After reading, she felt well enough to take a shower—something she had forsaken for the past four days which was totally out of character for her. Her appetite returned, the depression lifted and she was back to normal. Then God revealed to her what had happened.

On New Year's Eve she had attended a party in the home of a friend (a non-believer). The friend's aunt and her companion, both spiritualists, were also in attendance. It was obvious to them that my friend was a Christian and that she disagreed with them on the issue of Harry Potter; (they had been raving about one of the movies). When the aunt left, she leaned over and kissed my friend on the cheek and at that point a curse was placed on her. The result was several days of deep depression, an inability to pray or read the Bible and a loss of appetite—even for her beloved chocolate! What would have happened to her had she not been in a church that believes in the gifts of the Spirit and the reality of curses? When I prayed for her, the demons were cast out of her and she felt the jerking of her body as they departed.

Curses are real and powerful and we have a nation of young people and adults reading about them and wanting to learn more. Are we foolish enough to believe they won't use them to get their own way or for revenge against their enemies? And Christians, more and more, are going to be seen as the enemy as we stand for the truth of the Gospel. To say Jesus Christ is the only way to the Father when the rest of society is crying out for unity of all faiths in the face of terrorism, will make Christians look like narrow-minded bigots. We will suffer persecution and curses will fly against us. We need to be mindful of these things and pursue Jesus with wholehearted devotion, and then, we will have nothing to fear.

Truly we are living in the age spoken of by the prophet Isaiah when he said, "Arise, shine; for thy light is come, and the glory of the LORD is risen upon thee. For, behold, the darkness shall cover the earth, and gross darkness the people: but the LORD shall arise upon thee, and his glory shall be seen upon thee" (Isaiah 60:1,2).

CHAPTER TWO

The True

Let's look again at the first verse of our passage in Ezekiel 47:

> ... *forefront of the house stood toward the east, and the waters came down from under from the right side of the house, at the south side of the altar. (Ezekiel 47:1)*

Keeping in mind that the temple in this Ezekiel passage is a human being, this first verse shows us some things about how we are configured spiritually. Our house has a door, our house faces the east, it has an altar, a right (or south) side, and (as the next verse reveals) we also have a left (or north) side.

Our spiritual door is our heart. When Jesus says, "Behold, I stand at the door, and knock: if any man hear my voice, and open the door, I will come in to him, and will sup with him, and he with me" (Rev. 3:20), He is speaking about the door of our heart. A quick look at several Old Testament scriptures reveals that manifestations of God were often experienced at a door.

The Lord appeared to Abraham in the plains of Mamre as he sat in the door of his tent in the heat of the day (Gen. 18:1). Sarah was standing in the tent door when she heard the Lord say she would have a child in her old age. As Moses entered into the tabernacle, the cloudy pillar descended, and stood at the door of the tabernacle, and the Lord talked with Moses (Exod. 33:9). The people worshipped, every man in his tent door (Exod. 33:10).

These are just a few of the examples of experiencing God "at a door." It is with our heart that we are able to hear God and see into His kingdom. Our heart is the doorway to a deeper spiritual realm in Christ.

The altar symbolizes our willingness to forsake our lives in order to gain Christ. Christ will not be formed in us without an altar. Even as Abraham was willing to offer up his son Isaac on an altar at God's command, we too must be willing to sacrifice all things that Christ may be formed in us. We may feel that we are experiencing great loss, but actually we are gaining everything.

Other key aspects of our temple involve directions—east, south and north (west is not mentioned in this particular passage). As we think of our temple, our body, we need to learn the meaning of east, west, north and south because knowing spiritually what these mean can open our understanding to certain passages of Scripture.

East is the forefront or what we are facing. (We will speak more about this later.) The west represents what is behind. What I am about to say about south and north will probably seem unbelievable to most, but I am thoroughly convinced based on two things—my study of scripture and what I have witnessed firsthand in the SRA ministry (to be explained later)—that my deductions are accurate.

In the Hebrew, the "south" also means "the right side" or "the right hand." North also means "the left side" or "the left hand." Biblically speaking, our spirit is on the right side of our body and the soul is on the left. Most of us are right-handed but some are left-handed. When we commence to walk, the foot corresponding to the dominant hand will usually stride forth first. This shows us that in the natural, we have one side that is stronger than the other. In the unseen spiritual dimension of life, we also have a left and a right side with one side being stronger than the other.

As Christians, we have a two-sided nature—a carnal nature and a spiritual nature. A carnal Christian lives out of his soul and the spiritual Christian lives out of his spirit. When we were born again unto God, the Spirit of Christ came to dwell in our spirit. It is in the spirit side of our being that we commune with God, intuitively listen for his voice and obey the dictates of our conscience. The soul side of our nature is concerned with things of this world, self-preservation and meeting our needs through our own efforts rather than relying on Christ and trusting in him. One side of our nature will be stronger than the other based on our relationship with Christ and our willingness (or unwillingness) to deny our self that Christ may be formed in us. A brief look at a few scriptures will reveal that in a spiritual sense our spirit is on our right side and our soul is on our left.

Ecclesiastes 10:2 reveals, "A wise man's heart is at his right hand; but a fool's heart at his left." (Keep in mind that "hand" also means "side.") A wise Christian is one who lives out of his spirit, being motivated and making decisions based on the communion with Christ that takes place in his spirit on the right side. A foolish or carnal Christian is a person who lives out of his soul…making decisions and meeting his needs through his own natural understanding and self-effort on the left side.

Job says, "Behold, I go forward, but he is not there; and backward, but I cannot perceive him: on the left hand, where he doth work, but I cannot behold him: he hideth himself on the right hand, that I cannot see him" (Job 23:8,9). We know that when we are born again, the Holy Spirit comes to reside in our spirit. This is why Job could say that God hides himself on the right side—he dwells in our spirit but we are not able to see him or hear him as we would like.

Job said that God was at work on the left hand. It is in our soul that the most work needs to be done. When we live out of our soul, we see life from a human and natural perspective. We strive to fulfill God's mandates and life's basic needs through our own efforts according to our own natural understanding. Because we are basically concerned with self in our soul, all attempts at righteousness having their genesis in the soul will be tainted with impure motives.

Another interesting scripture concerning right and left is found in the New Testament where Jesus said, "Take heed that ye do not your alms before men, to be seen of them: otherwise ye have no reward of your Father which is in heaven. Therefore when thou doest thine alms, do not sound a trumpet before thee, as the hypocrites do in the synagogues and in the streets, that they may have glory of men. Verily I say unto you, they have their reward. But when thou doest alms, let not thy left hand know what thy right hand doeth, that thine alms may be in secret: and thy Father which seeth in secret himself shall reward thee openly" (Matt. 6:1-4).

Jesus was saying here that our giving should spring forth out of our spirit (the right hand) rather than our soul (the left hand). If we give from our spirit, we will be doing so at the unction of the Holy Spirit from a pure and righteous motive; then God will be able to reward us. If we give out of the soul, we will have an impure motive, desiring for others to know about our giving so they can admire and compliment us. The only reward we will receive then is carnal and fleeting. The true rewards come from God in response to our actions that spring forth from our spirit with pure, godly motives.

David said, "I have set the LORD always before me: because he is at my right hand *(side)*, I shall not be moved" (Ps. 16:8, italics mine); also, "The LORD is thy keeper: the LORD is thy shade upon thy right hand *(side)*" (Ps. 121:5). Here again we can see that the spirit appears to be on the right side. In the following section we will see how the Devil uses the principle of right/left sides for his evil purposes.

Having said all the above about the soul and spirit, I need to add that I don't believe spiritual realities are necessarily as distinct or black and white as I have explained them here. The truth is, there is a lot we don't know. Scripture contains depths where none have yet gone. The more I study, the more I realize I don't understand!

The Evil Division of Right Side/Left Side

When we are ministering to someone who has been highly programmed through satanic ritual abuse, there may come a time when they will experience extreme distress feeling as though they've been severed down the middle of their body from head to toe. This is a very physical, confusing and painful experience for them and needs to be ministered to immediately. At this time, the demon put in place through rituals to keep their soul separated from their spirit is beginning to manifest and must be cast out.

The Bible tells us in Hebrews 4:12 that the Word of God separates the soul from the spirit (a process more thoroughly explained in the following section), but in Satanism, a demon is called into the child to keep the soul separated from the spirit. God created us with our soul and spirit connected. Our soul relates to the natural world and our spirit to the spiritual realm; because of their connectedness, we don't see, hear and experience directly the spiritual realm around us.

God does not want us to see into the spirit realm because He knows we will see according to what is in our own heart. Because none of us has been perfected yet, we all have darkness in us. This darkness will enable any demons we see to deceive us. As the Bible says, Satan can appear as an angel of light. The most intelligent, highly educated person on earth is no match for a demon. They are incredibly intelligent, crafty and deceitful while at the same time being themselves deceived! Since beginning the ministry to satanically ritually abused persons, I have confronted and cast out large numbers of demons, yet with all this work in deliverance, I have only seen a demon during ministry one time. It was seen as a small, dark shadow that darted out of the room in a split second. Other than that, the only time I saw demons was over forty years ago when I was totally uninformed about the things of God and was actively delving into cult literature and ignorantly desiring forbidden supernatural experiences. These activities had begun to open my eyes to the spirit realm, but after I repented and sought the Lord with renewed fervor, I never saw demons again.

Andrew Jukes has interesting things to say about the spiritual realm around us:

Heaven is not far off. Heaven is our home. Nothing but our flesh, with its fallen self-hood and unbelief, hinder our seeing the kingdom which is at hand. For what is but the spirit-world of light, which is lost or shut to the natural man, only because by the fall the life of God is crushed, and spiritual sight and sense are gone, so that man though a spirit is content to live in earthly things, not indeed without cravings for the spirit-home, as every false religion and superstition testify, nor without ceaseless protests, in his yearnings, hopes, and fears, nay even in his very dreams, that the outward world is not the only one. For indeed man is a spirit, in a house of clay, and therefore, though he knows it not, is an inhabitant of an inward, as well as of an outward, world. Outwardly indeed, as in the present body and its life, we are in a world lighted only by the sun of nature, but inwardly our spirits even now are in a spirit-world, which only is not opened to the natural man, because to open it to such would be to open the dark world, into which by sin we all have fallen. But if by grace man is right with God,--if through Christ he is brought back in spirit from self-will and self-love to trust God,--the opening of the unseen only opens again the world of light and love, which is man's proper home and true dwelling-place. What therefore will be manifested to each man at his death may be anticipated here, and entered into more or less, just as we live in Christ, and Christ in us. Opening heaven is but opening the inward spiritual world, which mercifully is shut to us till we are restored to peace with God through Christ Jesus. (Jukes 1891, 14)

There are persons, however, who do see into the spirit realm even though they have not reached the state of spiritual maturity that is free of self-will and self-love. These persons are those who have been involved in Satanism and witchcraft to the extent that the veils separating them from that realm have been removed and there has been a separating of soul and spirit. These persons may be either perpetrators or satanically ritually abused persons. Even though the demon separating the soul and spirit is cast out, SRA persons are still incredibly sensitive to the spirit world, and they can be of great benefit to the church.

I know by experience that what I am about to say is absolutely true. Satanists and witches are able to walk into our churches and even climb to positions of power in our local churches and to national levels of power in our denominations because Christians lack the gift of discerning of spirits. It is impossible to detect these persons apart from the revelation of the Holy Spirit. They may be attractive in appearance, personable in conversation and know the Bible very well. They may have attended the same conferences we attend and read the same Christian books we've read. They will lift their hands in praise during our worship services and sing our songs even when the songs denigrate Satan. It is absolutely impossible to discern them by any natural faculty.

I am extremely grateful to the SRA persons in our church who have sounded the alarm for us many times. And I am extremely grateful to a holy and loving God who is beginning to open somewhat this realm to me. It is just beginning and only after a very long preparation (a lifetime? or so it seems!).

I'd like to elaborate a little on how my SRA friends are able to sound the alarm when witches or Satanists try to enter our fellowship undetected. Witches and Satanists get their powers from demons, and they carry a load of demons with them wherever they go. When one of these Satan worshippers enters a church, the demons they carry jump onto some of the people and start trying to influence them. The only people who feel them are the SRA people. Before we left our denomination and formed an organic home church, I often had to perform deliverance on one or two SRA persons after a church service where one or more of these evil persons had been in attendance.

What do we do when a witch or Satanist tries to become an integral part of our fellowship? When we were part of the organized church and in a denomination, there was very little we could do but pray. If we brought the truth out in the open, immature church members went behind our backs to our denominational overseers and our job was on the line! The denominations have to maintain their buildings, programs and salaries…all of which require money which comes from the parishioners. If God decides to remove some tares from the local church and they take their money with them, the pastor looks like a failure to the overseers. Additionally, many church leaders are not knowledgeable about the evil supernatural and tend to downplay it or ignore it. For these reasons, we found that we could not fully follow the Holy Spirit's leading while remaining in a denomination. God was able to lead us out in such a way that we were able to retain a good relationship with those in position over us. Now that we are in the organic church meeting in homes, when anyone wants to join us who has a wrong spirit, we are able to deal with it according to the Lord's leading.

While we were still a part of a denomination, there was one particular situation that comes to mind where a woman whom many discerned to be a witch had to be confronted as she was causing much damage to our people. She had been attending our church for only a few weeks and was causing a terrible ruckus amongst our severely abused persons. They were aware of demons and curses coming upon them whenever this woman was around. I would cast the demons out of them, and as they manifested they would threaten me and brag about how they would bring my ministry down through this woman. There was nothing I could do about it, they boasted, as I broke curses and cast them out.

I noticed she was complimenting me and trying to get close to me. One of the first times I met her, she wanted me to include her in my abuse ministry. She said she was an intercessor and that I should tell her about specific persons and situations in my ministry so she and her other intercessor friends (not in our church) could pray. I knew immediately this was not of the Lord.

There came a time when I had to confront her. My husband, who was the pastor, and one other person were in attendance. After opening with prayer, I said to her, "There are many abused persons in this church who are very sensitive to the spiritual realm. All of them are having a problem being around you. I was wondering if you could shed any light on this situation?"

She looked up at the ceiling and all around the room, saying nothing for a full minute. Then she said, "I know why...but I don't think I'm going to say anything about it. I'm planning to move on to another church, so I won't be around here any more."

That was it! The meeting was over and she went on her way. I honestly felt love for her. That poor woman is very deceived. Who knows, she may have been abused as a child. I know Jesus loves her and died for her, and I was thrilled to have felt His love for her. We continue to pray for those who have tried to bring harm to our people.

Around this time the Lord gave my husband a dream. In the dream God was telling him that the hurts and problems we had faced in previous churches were the direct result of witchcraft. How wonderful to finally be entering into the gift of discerning of spirits! The Lord has used many in our church to discern, as a group, those sent in by the evil one. There is a lot of safety in knowing we are all in agreement.

In many persons who have been satanically ritually abused, their soul and spirit have been separated freeing the spirit to become part of the spirit world with considerable access and awareness of that vast realm. This separation of soul and spirit is purposely done to make the child subject to the terror, pain and control of the demon spirits who then come in and rule over her. She feels their sharp claws digging into her awakened spiritual body, suffers the bites of their teeth, their beatings and their rapes. The terror of this is beyond anything imaginable and causes them to dissociate repeatedly into many parts often called "alternate personalities" or "alters" for short, or sometimes just called "parts."

Satanically ritually abused persons who have accepted Christ as their Savior usually experience more attacks and injury on the left side of their body than on the right side. This is because Christ's Spirit is in their spirit on the right side; therefore, demons and cultists cannot do as much damage there as they can on the left side. For years I was completely baffled by this phenomenon of "left side, right side" until God showed me the scriptures showing the spirit is on the right side and the soul on the left. The Lord is able to give more protection to their right side because that is where He dwells in greater proportion. They do horrible things to the body, soul and spirit of the ritually abused but there is a place in the spirit, where Christ dwells, they cannot touch. I'm not sure how literally this can be applied to persons who have not been satanically ritually abused, but this information can be very helpful to ministers who are helping SRA persons.

Different Temples

I explained that the healing waters are flowing out from the spirit of a believer. Most Christians are familiar with the passage in 1 Corinthians stating that our body is the temple of the Holy Spirit, but few stop to consider a non-Christian's body can be a pagan temple. Christians desire to be filled with the Spirit of God but Satanists desire to be filled with demons. During their rituals, they call demons into themselves with chants and various acts of perversion and cruelty. It is hard to believe human beings could actually desire to be filled with demons, but to them, demons are powers, and they want all the power they can get no matter what the cost—even if it means sacrificing their own children.

Satanists can gain a certain amount of power by calling demons directly into themselves, but the greatest powers come through the practice of satanic ritual abuse. In SRA a child or infant is chosen to be their special power source. (A girl or boy could be chosen for this, but it seems that more girls are chosen…at least more women seek counsel for this, so I will be using the feminine gender.) The most powerful demons are summoned into the child during rituals. People wanting the greatest powers must rape the child in order to get them. In this way, the Devil transfers his powers to his human agents to do his dastardly deeds and destroys the life of an innocent child in the process. As the child grows up, she remains in bondage and torment for the rest of her life or until set free through Christian ministry.

This horrendous abuse often begins when the baby is in her mother's womb. The most common method of torture is to insert needles into the mother's womb, a terrifying experience for the baby. During Christian ministry the Holy Spirit will give those so abused a vision of their experience in which they are able to release their pain and fear. Jesus comes, comforts and heals the little one so horribly violated.

Soon after birth the baby's vagina is cut open with a hot knife, and, of course, there is no anesthesia. This process is repeated over and over again in the early years of life. Perpetrators insert their fingers to stretch her little vagina until they are actually able to rape her before she reaches the age of two.

I hesitate to tell such horrible details, but those who minister need to understand how far back the abuse often goes and how totally fragile and broken these people really are. Each time such abuse occurred, they dissociated in order to bear it. They will have inside many little ones who need Jesus' most tender presence in order to heal. No secular counseling techniques can begin to reach the depths of such pain nor heal it.

Can a Christian Have a Demon?

The first workshop I conducted on the subject of satanic ritual abuse was challenged at the end by a man who held to the doctrine that a

Christian cannot have a demon. This was a painful experience for my dear SRA friend who had accompanied me to the conference. She knew she was not yet finished with her memories and still had demons within. This man was, in effect, saying she was not a Christian, when, in fact, she loves Jesus very much.

Picture, if you will, two little girls sitting together in a Sunday school class hearing the Gospel message of salvation. One child was raised by loving Christian parents and given every advantage in life. The other was born to parents who worship the Devil and was subjected to the horrendous abuse described above. Both children are touched by the message and ask Jesus into their heart. Can you imagine the Lord saying, I'll come into this one child because she does not have demons but I won't come to the other girl because she has demons? That doesn't sound like the Jesus I know!

Children subjected to such horrible abuse often cry out to Jesus for help and He comes to dwell in them in a special place in their spirit. Against their will they are forced to endure horrific, painful, humiliating rituals that fill them with powerful demons. Even though they have demons, the Lord will not leave them nor forsake them.

Jesus, being a God of love and compassion, would not refuse to come to a suffering child just because demons were being put into her against her will. He is the One who was criticized for eating with publicans and sinners and said, "They that are whole have no need of the physician, but they that are sick: I came not to call the righteous, but sinners to repentance" (Mark 2:17). To eat with publicans and sinners, who obviously would have had demons, is to be in the same house with them. The correlation is obvious—each of us is a house in which the Lord dwells by His Holy Spirit. If there are some evil spirits there, that doesn't keep the Lord from coming in to help the wounded person.

In the King James Version of the Bible, the word "possessed" in regards to demons could be a stumbling block for some persons. The Greek Word translated "possessed" is *daimonizomai*, meaning "to be exercised by a demon." Some believe it is more accurate to say a person is "demonized" rather than "possessed." Possessed implies ownership and demons cannot own a Christian.

In Matthew 16 we see Peter receiving and acting on information from both the Devil and God in the space of a few verses. In verse 16 Peter states that Jesus is the Christ, the Son of the living God. Jesus then exclaims that Peter has not spoken out of his own revelation but by direct revelation from God. In verse 22, after hearing Jesus speak of his impending death, Peter rebukes him by saying, "Be it far from thee, Lord: this shall not be unto thee." Jesus turned to Peter and said, "Get thee behind me, Satan: thou art an offense unto me." Jesus directly addresses Satan as He speaks to Peter, the one who has just had the revelation of Who He is!

Could Peter have had a demon in him? Maybe. Or perhaps one was whispering in his ear…maybe it was Satan himself. Whatever it was, it reveals how a person who loves Jesus can speak or act by revelation from God one minute and then speak on the Devil's behalf the next. This is often the case with those who have been satanically ritually abused. They can hear clearly from God and also from the enemy. This can be very confusing for them and for those around them. We must live by prayer and filter all things through Jesus.

One scripture quoted by those who believe a Christian cannot have a demon is in 2 Corinthians:

> *Be ye not unequally yoked together with unbelievers: for what fellowship hath righteousness with unrighteousness? and what communion hath light with darkness? And what concord hath Christ with Belial? or what part hath he that believeth with an infidel? And what agreement hath the temple of God with idols? for ye are the temple of the living God; as God hath said, I will dwell in them, and walk in them; and I will be their God, and they shall be my people (2 Cor. 6:14-16).*

Belial is an epithet for Satan. The word "concord" means "to be in harmony with." Jesus Christ will never be in harmony or fellowship with the Devil or any demon, but this does not mean He cannot come to an abused child and dwell in her spirit should she make this request. Demons are often called into an infant while still in the mother's womb, to say nothing of the horrible rituals done at birth. David said in Psalm 139, "If I make my bed in hell, behold, thou art there." If God can follow someone into hell, He can certainly come into a satanically ritually abused child who needs Him so desperately.

Many children abused in satanic cults hear the gospel at an early age. It is not at all uncommon for the cult family to be involved in a church and attend regularly. Sometimes the father is actually the pastor of a church and rituals are sometimes conducted in the church as a sacrilege to Christ. Although the child may not hear about Jesus from the parents or pastor, there is often a Sunday school teacher or some other person the Lord brings in to share the truth with the child. It only takes one time for these desperate children to remember who Jesus is and know to call upon Him in their suffering. So, as surprising as it may seem, it is not uncommon to see SRA persons who were raised in the church.

CHAPTER THREE

The North Side of the House

We have learned from the first verse of Ezekiel 47 that the Holy Spirit (waters) is flowing out of the spirit of the individual on the right, or south, side. Verse two will reveal what is happening on the north, or left side, regarding the soul.

> *Then brought he me out of the way of the gate northward, and led me about the way without unto the utter gate by the way that looketh eastward; and, behold, there ran out waters on the right side. (Ezekiel 47:2)*

This verse shows that the Holy Spirit is leading this person away from a manner of life wherein he walked according to the dictates of his soul (brought me out of the way of the gate northward). The word "way" means in Hebrew, "a course of life or a mode of action." The Hebrew word for "brought," *yatsa*, also means to "pluck up." Jesus is "plucking" him "up" and delivering him from this natural and earthly way of perceiving and living.

The person having this experience of entering into the fullness of Christ is a mature Christian…one who has been denying self, taking up his cross daily and following Christ. We know he is mature because His spirit is filled with living water to the point it is flowing out into the soul and, as will be seen later, into the physical body and all aspects of his being. This is not an experience for a carnal or immature Christian. In spite of this maturity, he still has a natural way of perceiving life based on the limitations he has always known. However, as the Spirit flows out into all his being, the Lord wants him to enter a more supernatural way of living.

Two gates are mentioned in this verse...the gate northward and the utter gate. A gate is an opening. In ancient times cities were surrounded by walls for protection and within these walls, gates were placed. Jerusalem had a wall with gates and the temple itself had gates.

The human body has gates—openings in the body—such as eyes, ears, mouth, etc., through which we perceive and partake of the natural world. The "gate northward" would refer to our natural senses that we use to inform us about our physical world. Jesus spoke of a different set of eyes and ears (gates) when He said, "For this people's heart is waxed gross, and their ears are dull of hearing, and their eyes they have closed; lest at any time they should see with their eyes and hear with their ears, and should understand with their heart, and should be converted, and I should heal them" (Matt. 13:15). He was saying that our heart has eyes and ears, and the condition of our heart determines whether or not we see or hear with understanding.

In our Ezekiel verse, Jesus leads him away from discerning life by his natural senses and brings him to "the utter gate," the gate that "looketh eastward." Since this gate is "looking" it must be the "eye gate." The word "utter" in Hebrew is *chemed* and means "beauty, desirable, pleasant." Jesus is leading this person out of his natural perspective to a more spiritual perspective as he learns to use the eyes of his heart. He is looking eastward toward a place where all things are beautiful and desirable. The Garden of Eden was in the East and Christ's return is said to be from the East (Matt. 24:27). These lovely things must be seen through spiritual eyes rather than the natural eyes.

As we focus the eyes of our heart on Jesus and His truth, our natural ways of thinking and perceiving will be discarded and we will find our soul being brought under the control of our spirit. We will no longer have a two-sided nature. Of course, only Jesus can do this in us, but we have our part to do. It is like taking the land. Every place the sole of our foot steps, He gives us—but we have to do the walking.

Watchman Nee teaches in his three-volume work, *The Spiritual Man*, that before the fall, Adam's spirit was dominant. The spirit reigned over the soul and the body. After sin entered in, the order was turned upside down with the body directing the soul and spirit. The spirit was least in authority. This is the configuration of a carnal Christian. However, when our life is surrendered to Jesus and we have experienced the fellowship of his sufferings via the transformational working of the cross, we will be brought to a new spiritual plain with the spirit ruling.

Our natural life needs to become supernatural. God wants to renew us in the spirit of our mind.

> *...put off concerning the former conversation the old man, which is corrupt according to the deceitful lusts; and be renewed in the spirit of your mind... put on the new man, which after God is created in righteousness and true holiness (Eph. 4:22-24).*

The mature Christian in the end times in whom the spirit of God is being released as a mighty healing river is one whose life has been brought to a place of servanthood and utter submission to Christ. Now God is taking him to a new place in Him reserved for the mature Church of the end times. He is bringing him to an open heaven and he is entering in.

When Philip brought Nathanael to Jesus in John One, Jesus exclaimed, "Behold an Israelite indeed, in whom is no guile!" There was no deceit (guile) in Nathanael and because of this he was able to see Jesus for who He really was, the Son of God. Due to the purity of Nathanael's heart Jesus was able to say to him, "Hereafter ye shall see heaven open, and the angels of God ascending and descending upon the Son of man."

Only the pure in heart can see God. If we are to become pure in heart, we must focus the eyes of our heart upon that which is perfect and pure—Jesus. We know He is with us because His Word tells us so. Now we must picture Him being with us. All day long, wherever we go, whatever we do, we must envision Jesus with us. This will help us become like the One on whom the eyes of our heart are focused. Not only are we to envision Jesus with us on earth, but also our self with Jesus in heaven. Looking toward the East is looking into heaven through the eyes of our heart.

What does heaven look like? Our purified imagination in conjunction with the Holy Spirit will create these visions as we endeavor to do so. When we see a picture of a beautiful earthly scene— whether it be a photograph or an artist's painting—we can put it into our inner world by remembering as many details as possible. Later, we can go there in our mind with Jesus and commune with Him.

When reading the gospels, imagine yourself being there with Jesus observing Him and picturing every scene in your mind with as much detail as possible. Imagine the setting, how the people are dressed, the expressions on their faces and the sound of their voices.

Any earthly scene can be turned into a heavenly one by perfecting it in our mind. We live in a cabin on the side of a mountain in the Finger Lakes region of New York. This area suffered a devastating ice storm in 1991 that literally tore the forests apart. Big trees were uprooted. Those that remained standing suffered broken limbs. Insects entered into the trees in the broken areas and have been eating their way down through the center of the trunks causing concern over the future of our forests and the logging industry.

In my heaven I envision our area in perfection with no downed or broken trees, the forest floor covered with lush green grass, delicate flowers scattered throughout and bushes covered with ripe, juicy blackberries. Gone are the ants, spiders and the pesky little gnats that fly up in one's face. Every beautiful place we make in our mind is a place to meet with Jesus. There we can talk with Him and interact with Him in our imagination as the Holy Spirit leads.

We may think that the Holy Spirit isn't really leading us, but when we are sincerely seeking God in our daily life, He is leading us more than we realize. I see His leading in unexpected ways. Others may consider these things coincidence, but I recognize the Lord's leading in them. For example, one time my husband and I were returning from a week's vacation and when we reached the town near our home, I asked him to stop at the local outdoor vegetable market so I could get some fresh produce. Not wanting to mess with my purse while shopping, I grabbed all the bills from my wallet and stuffed them in my pocket. In the process, a dime fell out onto the floor of the car. I stuffed it in my pocket and went into the market. I had three items in mind to buy… cabbage, apples and lettuce, but changed my mind about lettuce and bought peaches instead. I had not thought about the money I was spending. When I reached the cashier and he said it would be $12.10, I reached into my pocket and pulled out the roll of bills. It turned out to be twelve one dollar bills. And of course, the dime I had picked up off the floor and placed in my pocket made the exact amount…not one cent more or less.

Was that coincidence? No, God knew how much money I had. He had me change my mind from lettuce to peaches so the amount in my pocket would exactly coincide with the prices. He does things like this so we will know He is leading us and providing for us. And they were very good peaches…juicy and flavorful! He knew they would be a blessing to us.

The visions I have been describing are places of healing for our soul and body. Whenever I have a physical problem, I swim in the healing river with Jesus. I have combined a gospel story with the Ezekiel 47 River and experienced healing for my eyes. In John Nine Jesus spat on the ground, made clay of the spittle, anointed the blind man's eyes with the clay and told him to go wash in the pool of Siloam.

In my vision, Jesus and I are in the healing river together. He reaches down to the bottom of the river, brings up a handful of heavenly mud and places it over my eyes as I am floating on my back. I imagine the mud as being cream colored and sparkling with power. I spend time imagining the power going into my eyes and changing them. Then I pop my head down under the water, rinse it off and rise up exclaiming I can see everything perfectly.

I have imagined this or some variation of it hundreds of times. My eyes are not perfect yet as I still need corrective lenses, but I have been healed of cataracts. I had almost given up on driving at night because the starburst-like glare of headlights was incredibly confusing and I could no longer read the street signs. I can now see clearly to drive at night! I can read all the street signs and the glare of the headlights is almost completely gone!

The Lord has also healed me of hay fever and allergies to mold and cats. I was on antihistamines most of my life and allergy shots off and on through the years. My visions, along with scripture memorization and drawing closer to the Lord, have resulted in my healing from these problems.

I have learned that God often uses physical problems to speak to me. When we bought our mountain cabin almost two years ago, I got busy painting and decorating and slacked off ever so slightly from my time with God. I still spent hours with Him in the morning but I forsook my afternoon time with Him. I developed a terrible patch of eczema on the palm of my right hand—my dominant work hand! It took awhile for me to get the connection between my behavior and my malady. Once I corrected my heart and actions, the eczema cleared up (medicine hadn't phased it).

There was a seventeenth century French Carmelite lay brother called simply "Brother Lawrence" whose writings on living in the presence of God brought him national and international recognition. His duties at the community consisted mainly of working in the hospital kitchen where he kept his mind constantly focused on Jesus and was therefore always in His presence. Brother Lawrence remarked,

> ...I have come to a state wherein it would be as difficult for me not to think of God as it was at first to accustom myself to think of Him...The time of business does not differ with me from the time of prayer; and in the noise and clatter of my kitchen, while several persons are at the same time calling for different things, I possess God in as great a tranquility as if I were upon my knees at the blessed sacrament. (Lawrence and Laubach 1973, 102)

God wants to bring His people to such a place in this present day as Brother Lawrence experienced hundreds of years ago in his Carmelite community. With all the potentials for disaster looming on the horizon of our modern world, we need to have a place within where we can always find peace and comfort in the presence of Jesus.

Some Christians have been taught that the imagination is evil and should not be used. This is error! The imagination is a gift from God. All creativity springs forth from the imagination. We all use our imagination every day as it is part of our inner being. If we are not using it for good by purposely focusing it upon Jesus and His truth, our flesh is likely to entertain fears, doubts or other non-productive thoughts and images.

Oswald Chambers wrote of the importance of using our imagination with his comments regarding Isaiah 26:3, "Thou wilt keep him in perfect peace, whose mind (imagination) is stayed on thee:"

> Is your imagination stayed on God or is it starved? The starvation of the imagination is one of the most fruitful sources of exhaustion and sapping in a worker's life. If you have never used your imagination to put yourself before God, begin to do it now. It is no use waiting for God to come; you must put your imagination away from the face of idols and look unto Him

and be saved. Imagination is the greatest gift God has given us and it ought to be devoted entirely to Him. If you have been bringing every thought into captivity to the obedience of Christ, it will be one of the greatest assets to faith when the time of trial comes because your faith and the Spirit of God will work together. (Chambers February 11. Chambers' "imagination" was changed to "mind" by editors several years after the original publication in 1935.)

In another entry, Chambers again speaks of the imagination as related to a passage in Isaiah 40:26, "Lift up your eyes on high, and behold who hath created these things:"

The people of God in Isaiah's day had starved their imagination by looking on the face of idols, and Isaiah made them look up at the heavens, that is, he made them begin to use their imagination aright…

The test of spiritual concentration is bringing the imagination into captivity. Is your imagination looking on the face of an idol? Is the idol yourself: Your work?...If your imagination is starved, do not look back to your own experience; it is God Whom you need. Go right out of yourself, away from the face of your idols, away from everything that has been starving your imagination. Rouse yourself, take the gift that Isaiah gave the people, and deliberately turn your imagination to God.

One of the reasons of stultification in prayer is that there is no imagination, no power of putting ourselves deliberately before God…Imagination is the power God gives a saint to posit himself out of himself into relationships he never was in. (Chambers February 10)

Leanne Payne points out that the use of the imagination and symbol are necessary for getting truth from our head down into our heart. To not use the imagination is to...

> ...leave people vulnerable to non-Christian groups that have empathy for the unhealed psyche. Those heavily into Jungian spirituality, the New Age, or some other form of Neo-Gnosticism and paganism know the language of the heart. They recognize that this language is metaphoric and symbolic. They are not afraid to visualize. (Payne 1985, 180)

The Bible has much to say about the imagination. For example, Paul prayed in Ephesians 1:18 "that the eyes of our understanding would be enlightened." The Greek word for "understanding" used here is *dianoia*, which also can be translated "imagination." The Greek word for "enlightened," *photizo* also means "made to see." So Paul is actually praying for the eyes of our imagination to be made to see. Paul goes on to state what it is he is praying for us to see, "that ye may know what is the hope of his calling, and what the riches of the glory of his inheritance in the saints, and what is the exceeding greatness of his power to us-ward who believe, according to the working of his mighty power..."

We are to visualize our self becoming all that Christ called us to be. He wants us to imagine the riches and glory of heaven and His power flowing out into our lives and the lives of those to whom we minister. We are daily bombarded with false images straight from the pit of hell via the newspapers, radio, TV, movies, etc. We must purposely push those images out of our mind and use our imagination to focus on the Real. We become that upon which we focus our mind and imagination.

The imagination is going to play a vital role in helping us experience the presence of God. The Bible tells us Jesus spoke to the multitudes in parables and "without a parable spake he not unto them" (Matt. 13:34). A parable presents truth in the form of a picture story—the sower sowing seed, the mustard seed becoming a tree, a woman making bread, the treasure hid in a field, a net cast into the sea, etc. Each of these will form a picture in our mind if we are willing. Jesus presented great truths in an illustrative way that enabled those who had eyes to see to visualize truth in pictorial form. He knew that abstract words speak to our intellect but pictures touch our heart—our emotions—and it was Jesus' intent to reach our hearts with the Father's love and truth.

In 1 John 5:20 we are told, "And we know that the Son of God is come, and hath given us an understanding, that we may know him that is true..." There are ten different Greek words for our English word, "know," The first "know" in this passage is *eido* meaning "to see" from the root word, *optanomai*, meaning "to gaze with wide open eyes as at something remarkable." The word for "understanding," is *dianoia* which is also translated "imagination." The second word, "know," is *ginosko*, meaning "be aware of," "feel," "be sure." Putting these all together a new understanding of this passage begins to emerge something like this: We can see and gaze with wide open eyes at the remarkable appearance of Jesus Christ, the Son of God, because He has given us an imagination that we might be aware of Him, feel His presence and know Him of a surety. When our spiritual body has been awakened, we can literally feel this taking place. When I turn my imagination towards the Lord and look upon Him with the eyes of my heart, the feeling of His presence is greatly magnified. It is truly amazing.

Peter instructs us in 1 Peter 1:13 to, "...gird up the loins of your mind, be sober, and hope to the end for the grace that is to be brought unto you at the revelation of Jesus Christ." We see *dianoia* (imagination) used here again as the word translated "mind." The Greek word for "gird up" is *anazonnumi* from two other words—*aha* meaning "repetition" and *zonnumi* meaning "to bind about as with a belt." This gives us a picture of taking every thought captive to Christ—by binding our mind as with a belt to strengthen it—as we repeatedly use our imagination to envision God's grace and truth as revealed in Jesus.

Jesus said, "Thou shalt love the Lord thy God with all thy heart, and with all thy soul, and with all thy mind." Once again, the word used for mind is *dianoia*. How many of us ever think to love God with our imagination? Rather than just saying the words, I love you, how much better to picture loving Him in whatever way seems appropriate to the individual. For some it could be climbing up in His lap and calling Him, Daddy. For others it could be bowing before Him and pouring fragrant oil upon His feet. We are only limited by our imagination, which happens to be limitless!

As people were offering gifts to the Lord for the construction of Solomon's temple, David prayed, "O LORD God of Abraham, Isaac, and of Israel, our fathers, keep this for ever in the imagination of the thoughts of the heart of thy people, and prepare their heart unto thee" (1 Chron. 29:18). As we are preparing the temple of our heart for God's presence, the imagination helps us focus on that which is true, honest, lovely and worthy of praise—the Lord Jesus Himself.

Another powerful verse from the Old Testament is Isaiah 26:3, "Thou wilt keep him in perfect peace, whose mind is stayed on thee..." The Hebrew word for "mind" here is *yetser*, which also means "imagination." There have been occasions where I have been able to help persons who were hysterical and completely out of control by getting them to focus their imagination on Jesus. As they purposely centered their imagination on Him, they calmed down and got control of their emotions. If we train our imagination to picture Jesus daily as we worship and pray, then if great calamities come upon us (such as a terrorist strike or catastrophic storm, etc) we can go to a place of peace in our mind where we can find God. It is more than imagination.

Another Old Testament word for "imagination" is *hagah*, but it is usually translated "meditate."

- Ps. 1:2 But his delight is in the law of the LORD; and in his law doth he meditate day and night.

- Ps. 63:5, 6 My soul shall be satisfied as with marrow and fatness; and my mouth shall praise thee with joyful lips when I remember thee upon my bed, and meditate on thee in the night watches.
- Ps. 77:12 I will meditate also of all thy work, and talk of thy doings.
- Ps. 143:5 I remember the days of old; I meditate on all thy works; I muse on the work of thy hands.
- Josh. 1:8 This book of the law shall not depart out of thy mouth; but thou shalt meditate therein day and night, that thou mayest observe to do according to all that is written therein: for then thou shalt make thy way prosperous, and then thou shalt have good success.

Using our imagination can greatly enhance our time of prayer and fellowship with the Lord. Many of us have hardened our hearts to the point our spiritual eyes and ears no longer function as intended. The eyes and ears of our heart are weak from inactivity much the way a muscle in the physical body atrophies when not used. The way to strengthen our spiritual eyes and ears is to practice using our imagination a little each day. When we purpose to visualize the face of Jesus and the truths of His kingdom, we are actually putting on spiritual glasses that will enable us to see the things of God and enter into a deeper spiritual dimension in Him. As we imagine the sound of Jesus' voice and the music of heaven, our spiritual ears will be strengthened and enabled to hear more specific words from the Lord.

CHAPTER FOUR

The Evil Looking Eastward

Both Christians and Satanists are looking towards the East, the spiritual location of the Garden of Eden. Since the day Adam and Eve were cast out of the garden, humankind has been seeking a way to return to this paradise. All people long to be free from the penalties placed upon them as a consequence of Adam's and our own sin. Not only do we long for a life free from painful emotions, sickness and death, but we also hunger for the supernatural. The Christian chooses to depend on God to meet these needs, but the Satanist turns to the Devil believing he is truly god. All people are looking to something outside themselves, something supernatural, to meet their spiritual needs and thus they are looking towards the East.

Even as Christians are looking for the return of Christ, Satanists are expecting Satan to come in the form of the Antichrist. Both groups recognize the time is at hand for the battle of the ages to determine who will rule over the earth. We know the Devil has already been defeated and it is just a matter of time before Christ rules over all the earth, but cultists are deceived into believing the Antichrist will reign and give them positions of power, authority and great riches. Satanic cults have been networking and seeking positions of political, religious and economic power for many generations in preparation for their "takeover" of the world.

Christians anticipate the return of Christ with the departed saints to rule the earth, but cultists believe when the Antichrist rules, the Devil will resurrect those Satanists who have died and they will take their places of world leadership. It is common for rituals to be held in cemeteries where, at the peak of their powers, they believe they see the Devil resurrecting the dead from their graves. What they are actually seeing is the deceptive phenomenon of demons who appear as human beings rising up from the graves. In this way, Satan deceives his followers into believing he has the power to raise the dead.

All this only briefly satisfies their longing for supernatural experiences and proof of immortality and drives them to seek bigger and more powerful rituals. It becomes an addiction just like alcohol or drugs. It is their way of getting high, coping with boredom and pain and assuring their position of authority, power and immortality with the Devil. The law of diminishing returns functions here just as with any addiction. In order to maintain the same level of satisfaction, the sacrifices must become larger, more numerous and more wicked.

Satanists know much more about the imagination than Christians do. They know that through the imagination they come into contact with the spiritual world; therefore, they have developed this faculty of the mind purposely in order to see, hear and experience forbidden things. They know that participation in cult activities will bring demons in to activate their imagination and open to them new realms of supernatural excitement and power.

Many Christians have been afraid to use their imagination for fear of contacting evil spirits, but the fact is, we all use our imagination. If we do not train our imagination and fill it with godly meditations from the Scriptures, the enemy can use it to draw us into fear or vain imaginings. The imagination is a gift from God and it is from this faculty of the mind that creativity springs. God created us in His image; therefore, He had to first see us in His imagination before He created us. We, too, are to use our imagination by allowing the Holy Spirit to inspire it and fill it with good things as we work in cooperation with Him by meditating upon the Scriptures.

It is not uncommon for schoolteachers to lead their children in creative exercises for the purpose of developing the imagination in which they are encouraged to create an imaginary friend or helpful guide in their mind. This, of course, is wrong because it introduces them to the evil supernatural realm of demons. This practice, in combination with the reading of Harry Potter books, super hero cartoons, etc., is leading millions of our children straight into witchcraft. Most often, the teachers leading these activities have no idea about the spiritual ramifications of their actions.

Children who are chosen by the cult for satanic ritual abuse are purposely placed in painful situations where their only recourse for survival is their imagination. They may be placed in solitary confinement for days at a time, forbidden to have friends, and deprived of all love and touch. Their only escape is to develop an inner world with imaginary friends and pretend situations. Into this world the Satanists, through rituals, bring demons to force the isolated child to interact with them.

Magic Surgery

Satanists use a procedure known as "magic surgery" to enhance the imaginative powers of the child. They will drug or hypnotize her and then tell her they are operating on her to place a certain object inside. This object will be something used for the purpose of controlling her. It could be something small, like a walkie-talkie, or it could be something as large as a house. If it is large, she will be shown a small replica of the object but it will be something she is familiar with. People will gather around her dressed in operating-room garb making sure she sees the needles and scalpels in their hands, and the "surgery" begins. The child feels extreme pain, plenty of blood is spread around and after the "surgery" she is bandaged up for a few days believing fully that the object is now inside of her.

It is amazing to hear of the things that are "placed inside" via magic surgery. It can be anything in the physical world—even an entire town. The larger objects are usually places where the child has experienced abuse such as certain houses, castles, dungeons, prisons, etc. Bombs can be placed inside to explode should she ever talk about her abuse to anyone. An exploding bomb is actually a multitude of demons released in a person to cause her to destroy herself.

Satanists take advantage of the imaginative powers of the child for purposes of control, but the fact is if it were not for the imagination, the child would go completely insane from the abuse. During the abuse, the child begins to imagine she is not there. Using the imagination, she concentrates hard on being somewhere else and letting another person take the abuse in her place. At this point there is a split in the conscious process in which a group of mental activities breaks away from the main stream of consciousness and functions as a separate unit, as if belonging to another person. This is called "dissociation" or splitting into so-called alternate personalities known as "alters" or "parts." Some people refer to this as multiple personalities but it is really only one person splitting off from herself in order to survive. By the process of dissociation it is possible for a person to experience horrendous abuse and totally forget about it. The ability to do this varies from person to person.

The Satanists know their victim is splitting and use this to their advantage. Each alter the child forms is assigned a place in her inner world by her tormenters. The towns, houses, castles, dungeons, etc. placed into the inner world of her imagination during magic surgery are now the places where the alters are assigned to live. Demons guard each alter to keep her isolated and under the cult's control.

As the child dissociates during the torture, she may form four, five or more alters during one episode of abuse. The first alters will be the weakest ones. They will be assigned a place in a dungeon, perhaps, where they will be out of the way since the weaker ones are not much use to the cult. The stronger alters formed as the abuse continues contain more of the carnal sin nature.

Here we see the total perversion of God's way of working with our soul. He allows us to go through difficult experiences in life that expose our sin. As we repent and declare our willingness to embrace the cross and die to our sin, Jesus severs the carnality from us and destroys it leaving us purified in that area of our life. By contrast the cult forces severe abuse, psychological and physical, upon a little child that causes her to split off from herself until she forms an alternate personality part that is basically composed of sin nature who is willing to join the cult in their sinful practices. It is a literal rendering of "if you can't beat 'em, join 'em." In the most programmed abuse, the weaker or good alters are locked away in a dungeon or prison inside with demon guards making sure they never get a chance to do anything…the demons can even torture them.

The cult alters, those containing more of the sin nature and willing to advance the purposes of the cult, are given names and assigned certain duties to perform for the cult. Many of these duties involve making life totally miserable for their host person. These duties can be anything an evil imagination can devise, but here are just a few by way of example:

- If she enjoys anything, make sure she is punished for it by making her vomit.
- If anyone compliments her, be sure to tell her how ugly, stupid and selfish she is.
- If she starts talking about her abuse, don't let her drink water any more.
- If she starts talking about her abuse, make sure her bowels never move again.
- Be sure you keep her awake at night and never let her rest. This alter may be given, via magic surgery, several alarm clocks set to go off hourly all night long. It is her job to activate them. Demons actually "sound the alarm" to awaken her.
- Keep her obese by making sure she overeats and craves sweets.
- Never stop reminding her she is a failure in life and will never succeed at anything.

- Make sure she suffers with headaches continually. These alters will be given objects via magic surgery such as ropes to wrap tightly around her head, hammers for hitting her head, etc. (These remind me of an old television commercial for headache pain medicine!)
- Make voodoo dolls and stick pins in them to keep her in physical torment. (This all takes place in the inner world of the imagination but it actually affects the physical body.)

The alters assigned these tasks have the power to fulfill them because demons are working with them. It is a way of making a person agree with demons thereby giving them permission to torment them.

The Satanists will choose a child to be their special child because of probably several reasons, but the main one will be her ability to dissociate. Various people have differing abilities for this. The more quickly a child can split and the more thoroughly she can forget her abuse, the more valuable she will be to the cult. They want a child who can form more alters because the person with the most alters will also have the most demons, and more demons mean more power. The child is unaware that she has powers and any powers she has are used against her and accessed by her perpetrators.

When a child has an exceedingly high ability to dissociate, the news travels out to other satanic cults throughout the country. Word of this eventually reaches those highest up in the cult hierarchy who will come to visit the child to see just how "powerful" she is. If she is highly gifted in her dissociative ability, she will be chosen for specialized programming by professional programmers, psychologists and evil geniuses, who know just how to "fine tune" and enhance her abilities for use by those higher up in the cult. No expense is spared in their preparations of this child for power. She will be flown to places all over America for their specific purposes and also to many foreign countries.

Hopefully the explanation of these cult practices will awaken Christians to see how vital and powerful the imagination is. The recipients of this kind of abuse have an amazing ability to see, hear and feel Jesus Christ. During Christian prayer ministry, He appears to them, removes the magic surgery implants, casts out the demons, rescues the alters and heals them with amazing demonstrations of His love and divine personality. If an imagination can be so powerfully used for evil in the counterfeit of what God intended, just think of the power in the imagination to be used for good if we are willing to righteously activate it under the inspiration and guidance of the Holy Spirit.

The True Altar Within

So far regarding the first two verses of Ezekiel 47, we have learned that the temple is a mature Christian in the end times; we saw the living waters as the Holy Spirit; right side/left side were revealed as spirit and soul respectively; the door was our heart; the East represented heaven; and gates were natural senses and spiritual senses. One item I only mentioned briefly is the altar.

The altar represents the sacrifice of the cross in our life. Unless we are willing to deny our self, take up our cross daily and follow Christ, we will never come to completion. We were all born with a sin nature, and the only way to overcome that nature is to die to it. Jesus helps us with this by allowing us to experience circumstances in life that require a decision to either serve our idol of self or choose God's way and give up our own desires.

I remember being deeply touched by the testimony of friends regarding the near death of their first child. André and Linda had been childless for years and were told they would never have children. They were bicycling their way through the Alps one summer when Linda started feeling tired and was having difficulty getting over the steep mountain roads. Upon their return to America, she found out she was pregnant. The impossible had happened and in a few months she gave birth to a healthy baby boy. Their joy over the birth of this child soon turned to dismay when he suddenly became seriously ill and near death. No one knew what was wrong with the infant as all color drained out of him, and he went into a coma. Doctors did all they could but to no avail. At last they told the parents to prepare for the worst. Only God could save their child.

As André and Linda sat there in the hospital with heads bowed at the side of the baby's crib, they heard God speak, not in an audible voice, but clearly in their spirits they heard Him ask, Where is your treasure?

Immediately they knew what they had done. They had placed their love for this child over and above their love for God. They knelt and prayed there in the hospital and asked God's forgiveness for making an idol of their child. Then they placed him on the altar of their hearts and said, "God, He belongs to You. Do with him according to Your will." Within minutes, color returned to the baby, his eyes opened and he began to cry. In just a few hours they were able to leave the hospital with their healthy baby boy in their arms.

When we make godly choices in the midst of trying circumstances, God is able to circumcise our heart. He cuts away the sin nature and thereby purifies a portion of our soul. Another metaphor would be to say He allows us to go through a furnace of affliction so that He may purge out the dross and preserve the pure gold. We can identify with Paul when he said, "I am crucified with Christ, nevertheless I live, yet not I but Christ liveth in me. And the life that I now live in the flesh, I live by the faith of the Son of God who loved me and gave his life for me." This is the way to overcome all things and live a victorious life in Jesus Christ.

When God purifies us through trials, He is dealing with different aspects of our soul. Good things in our soul are mixed with impure motives. The working of the cross purifies our motives by discarding the sin nature and then preserving the purified part under the reign of our spirit. This is the process of sanctification...bringing all things in subjection to Christ in our spirit.

The Evil Perverted Altar

In satanic ritual abuse where victims are forced to endure horrendous trials of terror, pain, and suffering, there are no good choices allowed. The only decisions they can make are evil ones forced on them through torture and manipulation. The only way to survive is to divide off from their main stream of consciousness and somehow leave the abuse behind for another part of the personality to endure. Through this process demons, in cooperation with cult members, separate the good characteristics from the carnal nature, but the good characteristics are not transferred to the spirit. They remain in the soul in the form of alters (alternate personalities sometimes called parts, inside persons or IPs) who are locked away in the inner world in dungeons, prisons, or even baby nurseries (created by the cult through mind control programming) where demons keep watch over them and torment them. The bad, or carnal characteristics, rather than being burned up, remain in the form of cult alters whose evil characteristics are honed and trained by the cult for their wicked purposes.

SRA survivors, consequently, are divided in their soul over and over again to the point they are not allowed to form their own identity. Having no healthy concept of who they are, they become slaves to the demons and cult members and are unable to break away even though they may live apart from their perpetrators as adults. The dividing of the soul into separate alters, combined with the presence of demons called into them during rituals and psychological programming, keeps them under the cult's control even from a distance. The carnal parts of them, in the form of cult alters, can take control of them when cued by the demons, and take them out to rituals or perform assigned tasks without the good parts of them knowing anything took place.

Here we see that something created by God to be good—the process of severing the carnal nature from the soul and transferring the good characteristics over to the spirit—has been twisted and perverted by the Devil and his demons so that what was designed by God to deliver us and bring us into new freedom in Him, is used by demons to imprison the soul in an internal hell.

As Christians, we are called to lay our self-life on the internal altar, a living sacrifice unto God, as we say, Not my will but thy will be done. In this way, God can bless us and transform us into His image. In satanic ritual abuse, the persons become living sacrifices unto Satan and are kept in constant torment with few opportunities of freely using their own will. The freedom to choose is totally violated in the rituals as their decisions are forced through torture so that their will is not able to develop normally. (As a result, many people so abused are stubborn and controlling later in life.) As stated earlier they are placed in situations where evil is their only choice. The evil forced upon them is so great they have to divide into several personalities before one consisting of mainly sin nature comes forth that is able to do the evil forced upon them.

Their free will is further violated by the fact they are forced to make vows to serve Satan and do certain jobs assigned to them by the cult. These vows place them under vitiating curses that greatly diminish their quality of life and hinder their advancement in all areas of endeavor. These vows are made by alters under torture who are then locked away inaccessible to the survivor so she is totally unaware these vows were made, yet she is bound by them because demons are stationed with the alters to enforce the vows. The following are a few examples of vows:

- The vow to never cry prevents the release of painful emotions.
- A vow to never succeed in life will cause one to behave in ways to ensure failure.
- A vow to never love again will block meaningful relationships.
- A vow to commit suicide if she ever talks about the cult will endanger her life.
- A vow to never let anyone touch her makes any human contact uncomfortable.
- A vow to be subservient and submissive to the cult hinders her ability to defend herself.

Sometimes vows are behind physical problems. One woman started complaining that she felt like she was burning up. She looked flushed and her skin felt hot to my touch. Later in the course of her memory, it was revealed she had made a vow that if she ever talked, she would allow herself to be burned to death.

Cult programming of vows is usually reinforced by some kind of visual reinforcement. For example, one child alter remembered being punished for not cooperating with the cult members who were raping her. She was forced to make a vow that she would never fight them again, and then they slashed the throat of her pet rabbit as she held it in her arms. Reinforcing vows with brutality creates tremendous fear thereby increasing the cult's control over their victim.

Vows are often layered in that one particular vow may have been made many times by several different alters. In that way, the cult ensures their victim will not be released from her vow should a counselor happen to find one of the alters and break a particular vow because several others will have made the same vow.

Vows are reinforced by demons. During ministry, once a vow is uncovered, the survivor is sometimes unable to say the words necessary to break the vow until the demon guarding the vow is cast out. Once that demon has been cast out and the vow renounced, a few other demons connected to it may have to be removed.

Vows are not limited to the satanically ritually abused. All people consciously or unconsciously make vows while growing up that hinder them later in life. I have found them in my own life in spite of the fact I had a good home and loving parents. My mother was a friendly, outgoing person who knew no strangers. I was sometimes embarrassed by my mother's boldness. As an adult, I was plagued with the problem of timidity—a painful hindrance that I seemed powerless to overcome. God revealed to me that I had judged my mother for her boldness and made the vow, "I'll never be like my mother." That vow had locked me into timidity. Once the vow was broken and I repented of judging of my mother, I had a new boldness and freedom to relate in a social context.

In judging my mother and making an unconscious vow, I had violated two scriptural principles. "But let your communication be, Yea, yea; Nay, nay: for whatsoever is more than these cometh of evil" (Matt. 5:27). This principle is further stated in James 5:12, "But above all things, my brethren, swear not, neither by heaven, neither by the earth, neither by any other oath: but let your yea be yea; and your nay, nay; lest ye fall into condemnation." The other principle is found in Eph. 6:2,3, "Honor thy father and mother; which is the first commandment with promise; that it may be well with thee, and thou mayest live long on the earth." When we violate God's commandments, there are always consequences. It is important to ask the Holy Spirit to reveal these violations to us so we can repent and break curses put on our own life through our disobedience.

CHAPTER FIVE

The Man with the Measuring Line

And when the man that had the line in his hand went forth eastward, he measured a thousand cubits, and he brought me through the waters; the waters were to the ankles (Ezekiel 47:3).

The man here is Christ. He is the One who leads us and measures us according to His own perfect life. The man Jesus lived in the flesh here on earth and never committed one sin. He desires to bring us to the same level of perfection. This seems totally impossible, and so it is in the natural, but God can do all things in us and through us. All we have to do is die to our sin nature and our natural understanding, and let Him live in us. As we do so, we find abundant life. As the Scriptures say, "He who loses his life for my sake shall find it." True happiness and fulfillment come in laying down our own life. God will be taking His Church of the end times further into perfection than has ever been possible. His final judgment is coming upon this earth and is even now beginning. Not only is He judging everything in the world around us, but also He is judging us regarding every minuscule particle of carnality and sin nature. We must enter into His kingdom even while on this earth but we must be changed first so that this mortal may put on immortality.

In previous chapters of Ezekiel the man has been measuring the temple with a reed. According to the original Hebrew, the reed can be a plant that grows by the river and in marshes, or it can be a rod as taken from the branch of a tree, but either way it is something rigid. The temple being measured in Ezekiel is spiritual in nature in that a human life is being measured rather than a literal building. I believe the reed represents the written, unalterable Word of God applicable to all people of every age…past, present and future. The Word has always been and will always be the standard by which every Christian life is judged. It is rigid in that God does not bend or alter His standard of righteousness. We must all come up to His standard which is the perfect life of Jesus, the Pattern Son.

Here in Ezekiel 47, a line is being used for the first time for measuring the temple. A line is flexible and I believe represents personal words being spoken to this individual. This Hebrew word for line, *qav,* is also found in Psalm 19 "The heavens declare the glory of God; and the firmament showeth his handiwork. Day unto day uttereth speech, and night unto night showeth knowledge. There is no speech nor language, where their voice is not heard. Their line (*qav*) is gone out through all the earth, and their words to the end of the world." When we look up into the heavenlies on a clear night and see the moon and the stars in their constellations, we can't help but think of God while something deep inside of us marvels at the grandeur and vastness of our universe. The thoughts we have at that time are often personal words from God as He whispers in that still small voice whatever we are able to receive from Him.

This word, *qav,* is also found in Isaiah 28, "For precept must be upon precept, precept upon precept; line upon line (*qav*), line upon line; here a little, and there a little: For with stammering lips and another tongue will he speak to this people." These scriptures indicate that the line, *qav,* represents personal words from God to the believer.

We are going to need personal words from the Lord to lead us into this new dimension of Spirit. As the first individuals cross over into this realm, they will prophetically help others through. Dreams, visions and prophetic words will begin to lead us through these waters. Jesus desires to speak words of love to us. He longs for us to know how deeply personal and intimate our walk with Him can be. In this depth of relationship, we will joyously cast aside the idolatrous things of the flesh. To the love letters of Scripture (the written Word or the reed) will be added the intimate, loving, personal words of Jesus (the line) that will bind us to Him in new realms of ecstasy, intimacy and obedience. At this stage in the believer's walk, he will be searching his life eagerly looking for every little worldly thing he can cast off in order to facilitate his entering further into the manifest presence of Jesus.

The fact that the line is "in his hand" means it is in His power. God decides when we are ready for this experience and He initiates the words and the work. All is done by His power and at His direction. We must learn to yield to Him and depend upon Him for all things as we walk through these waters. Our own righteousness cannot lead us through the waters. Only by our willingness to give up all things will we be able to enter into this new depth of relationship with our Lord. He will become our all in all.

Measured

"He measured a thousand cubits, and he brought me through the waters." Jesus contained the Spirit of God without measure. "For he whom God hath sent speaketh the words of God: for God giveth not the Spirit by measure unto him" (John 3:34). However, we receive the Spirit by measure as we are able to receive Him. Some of the personal words we receive from the Lord will involve divesting our life of things that would prevent our receiving the fullness. Let me illustrate:

God may say, "I don't want you watching any more 'R' rated movies."

We say, "Okay, Lord," and get rid of our "R" rated DVDs. We make sure we flip to another channel whenever one comes on the television.

Then after awhile God says," I don't want you watching PG-13 movies either." And we comply.

Then He says, "I don't want you watching any movies. They are a waste of time. The days are evil; the time is short. I have other things for you to do."

We say, "Okay, Lord, no more movies for me. I'll just watch the news and nature programs like National Geographic."

However, it may not be long before He says, "I don't want you spending any time watching television. Your mind is being programmed with lies and propaganda."

If we are obedient, we give it all up and occupy ourselves with more productive things like increasing our Bible study time, reading good Christian literature and spending more time developing relationships. It may not be long before we find ourselves watching "God's TV" as dreams and visions begin to increase. This is how it is when we find ourselves going deeper and deeper into the Spirit. There is always something we need to forsake, but God has things for us that are far richer and more fulfilling than what we forfeit.

Webster defines "measure" as: "the extent, dimensions, capacity, etc. of anything, especially as determined by a standard." The standard to which we are being measured is Jesus. Little by little the Lord reveals to us areas of our character that need to be changed. As He does so, certain things in our life have to go. As those things go, we receive more of Him.

The Hebrew word for "measured", *madad*, also means "extended" or "stretched self." It is the same word used in 1 Kings 17:21 where Elijah "stretched himself upon the child three times," and the child "revived." The Holy Spirit gently falls upon the believer as Elijah came upon the dead child. Since my spiritual body has been awakened as I described in the first chapter, I have often felt the Spirit of God gently falling upon me. The Spirit feels as light as a feather...so sweet and tender that sometimes I hold my breath to make sure I can feel it to the fullest. I most often feel this when I lie down to rest.

When Elijah stretched himself over the child, the Spirit of God in Elijah came into the child bringing supernatural life into his body. There is a similar account in 2 Kings where Elisha stretched himself over a dead child, "...his mouth upon his mouth, and his eyes upon his eyes, and his hands upon his hands; and he stretched himself upon the child..." The Holy Spirit wants to come to us in the same way. He desires to overshadow us and merge into us—His eyes becoming our eyes, His hands becoming our hands, etc., in a total merging of two beings into one.

This can only be done "by measure." We can only receive the presence of God in small doses or measurements. There are two reasons for this, the first being that Almighty God is so phenomenally holy and powerful, we can only bear to receive Him a little at a time. Not only does He stretch Himself upon us as Elijah and Elisha did with the dead child, but also we ourselves have to be stretched in order to contain all that God desires to pour into us. In other words, our capacity to receive God has to be expanded to receive all of Himself that He longs to pour into us. I have also been able to feel this.

When Elijah stretched himself upon the dead child and he revived, the Hebrew word for "revived," *chayah*, also means "quickened." This brings to mind the New Testament passage in Romans 8:11, "But if the Spirit of him that raised up Jesus from the dead dwell in you, he that raised up Christ from the dead shall also quicken your mortal bodies by his Spirit that dwelleth in you." This is something God will be doing to our bodies as we progress further into the chaotic events preceding the return of Christ. Our bodies need to be quickened in order to rise up into the dimension of spiritual perception and health necessary to take us through the turbulent days ahead. Although I am not perfected, I have found myself enjoying increased strength, stamina and good health as I age. Usually people experience just the opposite.

The second reason we can only receive Him by measure is that self must be emptied out in order to receive Him. Each time we choose against self and yield ourselves more to the leading of the Holy Spirit, we empty out "space" that can in turn be filled with more of Christ.

This principle can be seen pictorially in the account of Elisha's raising of the dead child. When he first stretched himself upon the child, the child's flesh became warm, but this was only a partial reviving. The second time Elisha stretched himself upon the child, the child sneezed seven times and opened his eyes fully restored. A sneeze is something that removes impurities from our system in the natural. We need to cooperate with God in removing the spiritual impurities from our lives so we can receive more of Him and be revived.

Thousand

Numbers in Scripture have, in addition to their numerical value, a spiritual interpretation. We can determine this spiritual meaning by studying how each number is used throughout the whole Bible. The word, "thousand," in Scripture means "blessing," because God is "the faithful God, which keepeth covenant and mercy with them that love him and keep his commandments to a thousand generations." It also means "delivered," and "victorious in war," as evidenced in the following scriptures: "So there were delivered out of the thousands of Israel, a thousand of every tribe" (Num. 31:5), and "One man of you shall chase a thousand: for the LORD your God, he it is that fighteth for you, as he hath promised you" (Josh. 23:10).

Our greatest enemy is within us…within our soul and our body. As Jesus comes to the believer and stretches over him to extend His presence into every part of his being, He will impart His life to those areas of the believer where death has indwelt via the sin nature. This will bring blessings untold and will eventually result in total deliverance. It is only because of our sin nature we wrestle with doubts, fears and raging emotions. It is because of the sin nature our bodies are subjected to disease and aging. As we begin to merge with Jesus, as we become one with Him, (according to His prayer in John 17), we will find ourselves being lifted to new heights of victory over all areas of conflict and death.

"He measured a thousand cubits," means He extended His presence over the person (measured) for blessing and deliverance (thousand) which the person could only receive by measure (cubits). God can only give us little doses of His presence at a time. He is so holy and magnificent, we can only bear to receive a little of Him at a time. The more He comes into us, the more the flesh dies and the greater our capacity for Him becomes.

Waters to the Ankles

As His presence is imparted to us, the revelation of Who He is continues to grow within us as He brings us through the waters of His revelation to the ankles (v. 3b). The Hebrew word for ankles, *ephec*, means "cessation, i.e. an end (especially of the earth)."

It was fifteen years after I had the experience described in chapter one of this book that I realized this scripture is describing exactly what I experienced all those years ago! Jesus had said in the vision, "These feet will never touch the earth again" which is very similar to the definition of "ankles" in *Strong's Concordance* which states, "an end (especially of the earth)." That night the gentle, rhythmic feeling of his presence awakening my spiritual body began in my feet and moved upward. My life has not been the same since. This awakening opened a whole new era in my Christian life and changed my entire life forever.

The ecstasy and awe of this experience have never left me because the feeling of his presence has remained and intensified. This experience prepares us for God's further work in us to bring us to a total end of self where the things of this world will no longer interfere in our relationship with Him. The awakening of the spiritual body enables us to feel the Lord's touch. I often feel His presence coming ever so gently onto my right shoulder. He has instructed me that when I feel this I am to picture his hand on my shoulder in my imagination. When I do, the feeling intensifies.

The words of an old hymn come to mind:

Turn your eyes upon Jesus,
Look full in His wonderful face;
And the things of earth will grow strangely dim
In the light of His glory and grace.

These words express the inevitable response of one feeling the Lord's awesome presence. As we continue down the river of God, our eyes are to be opened that we may look toward the East and behold Christ coming to us in a new dimension. The awakening of our spiritual mind very much involves learning to use our imagination. Paul prayed in Ephesians One that God would give us "...a spirit of wisdom and revelation in the knowledge of him," that the "eyes of our understanding" (imagination in Greek) might be "enlightened" (made to see).

For our protection, God has allowed "veils" to be placed between us and the spiritual realm because we are only capable of seeing according to what is in our own heart. If there is darkness in our heart, we will see the evil of Satan's spiritual realm. This can only lead to deception. God will remove these veils for us as we die to everything of this world; then we will no longer be susceptible to deception.

We overcome darkness in the same way our Lord Jesus did as expressed in Hebrews 2:14 "Forasmuch then as the children are partakers of flesh and blood, he also himself likewise took part of the same; that through death he might destroy him that had the power of death, that is, the devil." Jesus overcame the Devil for us by his physical death. We must overcome him with our death to carnality. Our sinful, carnal nature is the only thing in us that allows the Devil to attack us. When the sin nature is totally dead, we will then be able to see into the heavenly realms without being deceived. Thomas á Kempis wrote regarding the cross:

> In the cross is salvation, in the cross is life, in the cross is protection against our enemies, in the cross is infusion of heavenly sweetness, in the cross is strength of mind, in the cross joy of spirit, in the cross the height of virtue, in the cross the perfection of holiness. There is no salvation of the soul, or hope of everlasting life, but in the cross. Take up therefore your cross and follow Jesus (Luke 14:27), and you shall go into life everlasting. He went before, bearing His cross (John 19:17), and died for you on the cross; that you also may bear your cross and desire to die on the cross. For if you be dead with Him, you shall also in like manner live with Him (Gal. 2:20; Rom. 6:8). And if you share His punishment, you shall also share His glory (II Cor. 1:5).
>
> Behold, in the cross all consists, and in our dying thereon all lies! For there is no other way unto life, and unto true inward peace, but the way of the cross and of daily mortification. Walk where you will, seek whatever you will, you shall not find a higher way above, nor a safer way below, than the way of the cross.
>
> Dispose and order all things according to your will and judgment, and you shall find that you must always suffer somewhat, either willingly or against your will, and so you shall ever find the cross. For either you shall feel pain in the body, or suffer tribulation of spirit in the soul. Sometimes you shall be forsaken of God, sometimes you shall be troubled by your neighbor; and, what is more, oftentimes you shall be wearisome to your own self. Neither can you be delivered or eased by any remedy or comfort; but so long as it pleases God you ought to bear it. For God will have you learn to suffer tribulation without comfort; and that you subject yourself wholly to Him,

and by tribulation become more humble. No man so feels in his heart the passion of Christ as he who suffers.

The cross therefore is always ready, and everywhere waits for you. You cannot escape it wherever you run; for wherever you go you carry yourself with you, and shall ever find yourself. Turn above, turn below, turn without, turn within, and in all these places you shall find the cross. And everywhere of necessity you must hold fast patience if you will have inward peace, and win an everlasting crown. (á Kempis 1952, 86)

The Perversion of Death to Self

The Devil takes the great truth of the cross and perverts it into a total opposite. God's purpose is for believers to deny their selfish sinful nature, but Satan's goal for his followers is for them to revel in self. Their philosophy is, "If it feels good, do it. Take everything for yourself no matter how many people you trample underfoot in the process." This philosophy taken to the extreme leads to human sacrifice.

Rather than deny self, the Devil has his followers deny others their very life by murdering them on an altar to Satan. Taking another person's life is the Devil's way of granting someone power! The more lives they can sacrifice, the greater the power they will have. Of course, this is all a great deception. They may gain power in politics, business, etc., but they will eventually find themselves totally powerless in the Devil's hands as they plummet into a hell far worse then anything imaginable. If Jesus said it would be better to pluck out our eye or cut off our hand than to go there, it has to be horrific.

In addition to the literal taking of a human life in ritual sacrifices, there is also the SRA person who is alive in body but whose life is a living death. Everything possible is done to make sure this person has no joy or comfort in any aspect of life. Programming and tortures are administered to make sure she cannot enjoy eating, sleeping, working, playing, relationships or anything else that makes life seem worthwhile. There is no rest or comfort for these souls.

How many satanically ritually abused persons are there in the world? In America? In your city...your church? No one knows the number, and it would be impossible to determine even through a census because many such abused persons don't remember their abuse. God in his infinite mercy enabled them to forget what happened, even though it still has an adverse effect on their lives. Others do remember and the horror is beyond description. They suffer greatly because of it. Although we will never know how many have suffered this abuse, the Lord has shown me something in His Word that indicates multitudes must have been so abused and are still being abused. Let me explain.

Anyone who knows anything about Satanism knows that they kill animals and people in order to get power or appeasement from the Devil. What people don't know is that there must also be a living sacrifice...a person who suffers greatly at their hands but does not die a physical death. This person's life is a living death, so to speak. These are the satanically ritually abused who live and work among us and desperately need our help.

Here is what the Lord has shown me. Power must come through death. The most powerful event that ever happened in the history of the world was the death and resurrection of Jesus Christ. Hebrews 2:14, 15 states, "Forasmuch then as the children are partakers of flesh and blood, he also himself likewise took part of the same; that through death he might destroy him that had the power of death, that is, the devil; and deliver them who through fear of death were all their lifetime subject to bondage."

When Almighty God chose to become a man and walk among us in flesh and blood and then willingly suffered and laid down His life for us, the greatest power of all-time was unleashed. This power destroyed the Devil and set free forever all those who choose to believe in Jesus Christ as the Son of God. There is nothing more powerful than this—no atomic bomb, hydrogen bomb, tsunami—nothing has ever been or will ever be as powerful as this. (Some of us may have a hard time believing the Devil has been destroyed, but the Bible says it, so it has to be true. The Devil can only have power over those he is able to deceive into believing he has power. Once we know the truth, he cannot affect us. Our greatest enemy is really our own flesh!)

It has always been God's plan for those of us who believe in Jesus to walk in this same overcoming power. We are to appropriate this power in the same way Jesus did, by laying down our life. However, it is not our physical life that we forfeit but our SELF life. Jesus said, "Whosoever will come after me, let him deny himself, and take up his cross, and follow me" (Mark 8:34). This command is in all three synoptic gospels. We will have no power at all in our Christian walk if we refuse this command. This is why much of the Church in America has appeared to be weak in the eyes of the world. When we seek blessing and prosperity but refuse the work of the cross in our lives, we have nothing to say to our society...we have no power to convict the lost of their sin or to minister life to anyone.

It is the cross, the total death to the sin nature, that will bring us into the greatest blessings ever known by any human on earth. No wonder there is such an attempt by the enemy to entice the church to seek after blessing and prosperity and neglect the cross. The Devil doesn't care if we prosper. He gets really scared when we embrace the cross, because he knows this will bring the power of Almighty God into everyday life here on earth and his plans will be foiled.

God made the rules and everyone, even Satan and his followers, must abide by God's laws to a certain extent. God has established in His Eternal Word that spiritual power can only come to a human being by the denying of the self life. No Satanist would ever deny himself anything since the very essence of Satanism is to get all one can for oneself and with no concern for the people one hurts in the process. Here's how they get around this principle of self denial.

They choose someone else to be the one whose self life is denied. This becomes the satanically ritually abused person. They choose a little child or baby and abuse that person to the point she is totally confused and denied any pleasure of living whatsoever. During painful rituals demons from hell are summoned into the person chosen to be the living sacrifice. She is denied her self life, she is the one who suffers the pains of a living death and therefore she is the one who can receive spiritual powers. Rather than receiving the life of Jesus as God intended, she is filled with demons...powerful demons...principalities, powers and spirits of wickedness in high places take up residence in her. She is so confused because of mind control and torture, she doesn't even realize she has these powers. (It happens to boys too, but more to girls hence I am using the feminine gender.)

The Satanists then take these powers from her by utilizing another principle laid down by God and intended only for marriage...that the two become one flesh through their sexual union. Paul states in 1 Corinthians 6:16, "What? know ye not that he which is joined to an harlot is one body? for two, saith he, shall be one flesh." They take a little child against her will, fill her with powers and steal the powers through rape and perverted sex acts. She is denied her life; they become one with her and take the "benefits" of her suffering.

Let's look again at this principle of the cross as found in the book of Romans: "I beseech you therefore, brethren, by the mercies of God, that ye present your bodies a living sacrifice, holy, acceptable unto God, which is your reasonable service. And be not conformed to this world: but be ye transformed by the renewing of your mind, that ye may prove what is that good, and acceptable, and perfect will of God" (Rom. 12:1, 2).

Satanic ritual abuse does the exact opposite. Rather than their mind being renewed, persons are tortured and tormented till their soul splits into many separate parts that are locked up in unreachable places deep within. These parts (alters) are tormented by demons and by horrific memories of abuse. Their bodies become riddled with sickness and pain. Their life becomes a miserable prison that is the exact opposite of what God intended for them through Jesus Christ.

Once we realize that the greatest satanic powers can only be utilized by accessing the powers of the person chosen to be the living sacrifice, we can begin to get an idea of how many persons must have been abused in satanic cults. Every satanic group needs its living sacrifice. Everyone in the group wants power. They get limited powers by participating in a ritual but the greatest powers come through sexually abusing the living sacrifice (the SRA person). This is why so often in memories of ritual abuse, the SRA person recalls the cult trying to make her kill the victim. She most often refuses and the Lord shows a picture of one of the perpetrators with his hand over her hand plunging the knife into the victim. They want her to commit this crime so that more demons will come into her thereby increasing her powers. Usually the last thing that takes place at the ritual is the rape of the living sacrifice. They want to keep her alive; therefore, the number of those allowed to abuse her in this way is limited because it is possible to rape a person to death.

When there is no victim to sacrifice at their ritual, they can still get powers by abusing their living sacrifice. They also access her powers when not at a ritual. This is why many persons who suffered such abuse have memories of multiple rapes. If the SRA person was raised in a satanic family where Satanism was passed down through the generations, her abuse will be phenomenal. I remember one woman I ministered to and brought into wholeness in Jesus Christ. She had a father, three brothers, seven uncles, a grandfather and many others who wanted her powers. Abuse took place daily. Her mother, who was also satanically ritually abused, was forbidden to show her daughter any love or comfort.

How does a person so severely abused survive? They are usually highly gifted, creative and intelligent persons. They dissociate in order to forget their tragic experiences. They also use their imagination to create a storybook family and live in a make-believe world of fantasy. They are often able to completely forget what happened.

So the answer to our question of how many persons have been satanically ritually abused has to be answered as multitudes. I'm just one person but over the past twenty years I have been astounded at the number of people living around me that I know personally who exhibit multiple symptoms of satanic ritual abuse. They keep walking into our church. My ministry is never advertised and I don't talk much about it, and still I know many of these people. I get many letters from them over the Internet.

If they are in my church, they're in your church. Some of them don't go to church, but if your eyes are open to understand the signs of such abuse, you'll see them many places. They need our help. If we are willing to lay down our self life in order to be like Jesus, we can minister to them in the supernatural power of Jesus Christ. It does require sacrifice, and we must be certain that God has called us into this ministry before we try to do it. For those of us so called, the rewards are incredible. The joy of seeing someone set free is far greater than anything we could experience in a life lived for self gratification… and the best part is, we get more of Jesus!

Waters to the Knees

We have seen that in these end times the water coming up to the ankles is a type of the presence of God coming to a person and awakening their spiritual body. This is an experience reserved for the Church of the end times heralding the beginning stage of the return of Christ. This next verse reveals more:

> *Again he measured a thousand, and brought me through the waters; the waters were to the knees. Again he measured a thousand, and brought me through; the waters were to the loins. (Ezekiel 47:4)*

When the gentle, tingly rhythmic feeling started in my feet, it quickly spread up to my knees and continued up over my entire body in a matter of seconds. The Hebrew word for "knees," *berek*, is from the root word, *barak*, meaning "to kneel," "to bless God as an act of adoration," "praise."

Once one has had this experience with the Lord, one can't help but want to worship Him. Worship intensifies the feeling of His presence. Waves of adoration, love and praise will sweep over us as we glory in the overwhelming sensation of His presence and love. Depths of worship and intimacy never before known to us will be our daily experience. This level of experience will not be limited to our regular prayer time or corporate worship. This presence will be something we feel all day every day no matter where we are. However, it will always intensify whenever we turn our thoughts and imagination towards the Lord.

The use of our imagination will greatly enhance our worship experience. If our worship consists of only words and songs, we are limited in how long or where we can worship. I can only say, "I worship you. I love you. You are worthy of honor and glory, etc." for so long and then I run out of things to say or it seems like vain repetition. But when I start to picture Jesus and see myself bowing before Him, when I visualize the nail prints in His hands and feet and see the love He has for me in His eyes, worship enters a whole new dimension. As we enter these waters to the knees, our expression and experience of worship will take on a whole new dimension and depth leading us further through the waters to our loins.

Waters to the Knees—Satan Worship

Being intensely jealous of God, Satan wants the whole world to bow in adoration and worship of him. The more mankind feeds his own selfish sinful nature, the more willing he becomes to worship and sacrifice to Satan. We need to remember that Satan's only access to humanity is through our carnal nature. One who has died to this is totally not affected by the Devil, his demons or any curses. This is why a man who is willing to lose his life for Christ's sake will actually save his life, and those who walk in holiness will not succumb to the Devil's tactics.

As wickedness abounds in our land, it will become increasingly important to walk in holiness for only then will we have God's protection. God desires to protect all His people but if we walk according to the dictates of our flesh, we will fall into the Devil's traps. Today, in this age of chaos, tyranny, and disintegration of our society, walking in the flesh may mean the actual loss of our very life. God will lead us by His Spirit as we deny ourselves, take up our cross and follow Him in a life of worship and adoration. As we live in His presence, we will truly be in the "secret place of the most High…under the shadow of the Almighty."

The Devil likes for his people to worship him in their satanic rituals with their sacrifices and praises. They bow down to Satan, shout and cry praises to his name. After a human or animal sacrifice, demons come into the people and empower them to worship Satan by becoming more evil and perverted. At this time in their rituals, they go into frenzied activities with sexual orgies and eating of human flesh, often tearing at it with their teeth like wild animals. All humanness is gone from the people at this point as demons completely take over their bodies.

Sometimes Satan himself shows up at a ritual even though he can only be in one place at a time. In total mockery of the Church being the bride of Christ, Satan forces many satanically ritually abused little girls to partake of a marriage ceremony with him after which he rapes them. There are no words to express the hideousness of this appalling counterfeit and mockery of the sweet oneness of Christ and His bride, the Church.

Waters to the Loins

The presence of Jesus continues coming down upon the believer as, "he measured a thousand and brought me through; the waters were to the loins" (v. 4b). The Hebrew word for "loins" gives the meaning as being "the waist or small of the back" and "side." This was literally true for me when the awakening began in my feet, came up to my knees and then spread over the trunk of my body which included my back and both sides.

However, as I stated in Chapter 3, there is another way of looking at this word "loins" as revealed in the New Testament where we read, "gird up the loins of your mind" (1 Peter 1:13). The Greek word for "mind" used here in 1 Peter is *dianoia*, which also means "imagination," and the word "loins," *osphus*, means "procreative power." The word "gird," *anazonnumi*, is a combination of the prefix, *ana*, meaning "repetition," "intensity," and "reversal," and *zonnumi*, meaning "to bind about especially with a belt."

There is a great spiritual teaching revealed in this one phrase, "gird up the loins of your mind," or as we could say, "Bind up, as with a belt, the procreative power of your imagination." The imagination is a function of the mind, a function that has a tendency to run wild if not purposely trained to remain under the control of the Holy Spirit. It is in the imagination we begin to wonder, "What will happen if this or that occurs?" and then worry and anxiety come in to darken our minds. It is in our imagination that we make "mountains out of molehills."

As we begin to use our imagination to visualize Jesus and the truths of Scripture, we will find our mind wandering off to other subjects. When this happens, we must "gird it with a belt" and bring it back to the spiritual subject we are picturing. As revealed in the prefix, *ana*, this must be done with repetition and intensity until we are able to reverse the wild wandering of our mind and bring it into subjection to the mind of Christ. With practice, our procreative powers are exercised and the imagination is built up to become a powerful vehicle for the expression of God to us personally and then out to others in the form of gifts of the Spirit.

The Old Testament word for loins used here is *mothen*, meaning "side." As I mentioned previously, both sides of my body were awakened as the feeling moved up from my feet to my knees and over my entire body. However, there is another side of me that was also being awakened as I was to learn later and that was my spiritual mind. The Lord has been showing me that we have a side of our mind we don't use. In these last days as the Lord comes upon His people, He is going to be awakening the parts of our mind that have never been used!

These healing waters will be flowing into the vast, unused portion of our mind awakening it to the things of the Spirit. It has been said that we use only ten percent of our brain. Surely God intends for us to use the other ninety percent. He created it for a purpose and I believe it was for these last days as we enter into His fullness. Based on the above-mentioned New Testament scriptures and some of my other studies, I believe that this unused portion of the brain has to do with the spiritual and creative parts of us. It is impossible to know all the implications of this but the possibilities are fascinating. We, the Church of the last days, are going to experience and know things beyond anything humankind has known in all of human existence until now. (This subject will be further explored in the section entitled "Brink of the River.")

If we are to experience expanded usage of our mind, it will only be as we partake of God's holiness. I believe God has not allowed the use of the other ninety percent of our mind because of the evil sin nature in us. We might misuse the power of our brain so God must wait until we are perfected in holiness to allow that part of our brain to function.

What we allow into our mind is of supreme importance. David said in Psalm 101:3, "I will set no wicked thing before mine eyes: I hate the work of them that turn aside; it shall not cleave to me." David knew that whatever he chose to look upon would put into his mind something that would remain there and influence his life. We are greatly deceived if we think we can watch an evening of typical American television and not be adversely affected by it. It is possible that we would eventually do or become like that upon which we focus. We may not see ourselves doing the same outward things we view, but we pick up sinful attitudes and our hearts become hardened to the things of God. Only a hardened heart can enjoy seeing people murder one another or commit adultery. It may only be acting but we find ourselves crying when it is sad or sitting on the edge of our chair during sustained intensity dramas. We are affected by television and movies in many ways we are not aware of.

Every time we turn on the TV, listen to the radio or read a magazine, we are often being exposed to powerful propaganda techniques devised by wicked profiteers based upon their knowledge of human behavior gleaned from modern psychiatry. They know the deepest longings of the human heart and play upon these unconscious desires in order to manipulate us to buy their products. Not only are they selling products, but they are also selling ideas and beliefs. As David Kupelian writes:

> The plain truth is, within the space of our lifetimes, much of what Americans once almost universally abhorred has been packaged, perfumed, gift-wrapped, and sold to us as though it had great value. By skillfully playing on our deeply felt national values of fairness, generosity, and tolerance, these marketers have persuaded us to embrace as enlightened and noble that which all previous generations since America's founding regarded as grossly self-destructive—in a word, evil. (Kupelian 2005, 11)

Waters to the Loins—the Mind of Evil

Just as God quickens unused portions of minds of Christians to enable them to perceive and participate in the deeper revelations of God, the evil one awakens the minds of his followers. The minds of evil geniuses combine with satanic forces to bring forth unspeakable wickedness. Every new scientific discovery that could be used for good is perverted into something evil to further Satan's kingdom on earth, e.g. evil weaponry, microchips, surveillance equipment and techniques, medical atrocities and every conceivable scheme for the torment, control and annihilation of humankind. Much of today's technology is being used to enslave the minds of our youth and dictate fallacious beliefs to the masses. Only those who walk closely with Jesus Christ can escape the proliferation of lies and deception aimed at the minds of everyone in the world today.

There is a part of our mind that no one knew much about prior to Sigmund Freud's discoveries regarding the unconscious mind. One morning during my time of prayer and Bible study, the Lord revealed something to me…that satanic ritual abuse *in its present form* did not exist before the discoveries of Sigmund Freud.

Satanic ritual abuse is seen throughout the Old Testament as making sons or daughters "pass through the fire." Child sacrifice to idols has been practiced since the Fall of man, but what we see today in satanic ritual abuse with its deliberate and elaborate programming schemes of the inner world were not possible before the discovery of the unconscious mind with its various defense mechanisms. Freud's concept of repression was said to be one of his major contributions toward understanding psychological processes. His daughter Anna wrote at length about repression and other defense mechanisms such as dissociation in her work, *The Ego and Mechanisms of Defense.*

Freud believed there had to be the existence of mental phenomena which was not available to awareness, but still had a powerful influence on mental life. He wrote that repressed material was not static while in the unconscious state, but rather had a life of its own and that such material developed more quickly and vigorously than material that was governed by the constraints and reality testing of conscious experience.

These discoveries were seized upon by evil geniuses of Hitler's Third Reich and used for experimentation on the minds of infants and small children for purposes of control and satanic power. Hence we see today in SRA the layering of the unconscious mind with alters created through severe abuse who control the conscious mind of an individual without his/her knowledge. In this way, parts of a person's mind that were programmed through abuse (and reside in the unconscious mind) are able to surface and cause the person to do things they would not ordinarily do when living out of their conscious mind. For example, a satanically ritually abused person with complex programming and control devices deliberately formed in the unconscious mind can go to bed at night, be awakened and taken out to a satanic ritual by a programmed alter in the lower recesses of the mind, come home and go back to bed and awaken in the morning without knowing he went anywhere during the night.

Freud wrote that the unconscious was composed of wishes and desires, impulses and drives, where reality had no place and there were no constraints on desire. One can easily see how this concept could be used to take advantage of a person's natural instincts for survival imbedded in the sin nature. Through dissociation certain splits in the psyche could be programmed to do evil without constraint because, as Freud wrote, the unconscious is in opposition to the world of order and common-sense and a great subverter of every day life.

According to Freud, because repressed ideas lie outside of consciousness, they cannot be easily controlled by it and are instead the source of many behaviors and experiences which do not have the character of being willed by the self. This concept was utilized by evil geniuses to program the mind of an SRA person to work against himself. Thus certain alters can be assigned the job of keeping the host person awake all night, giving him headaches, telling him he is inferior to everyone else, calling the cult to tell them the location where he has fled for safety, etc. These perpetrators took advantage of Freud's discoveries to harness the unconscious mind of an individual in order to control him and serve the cult against his own conscious will. However, there is more than psychology involved here. The spiritual dimension of demons is added into the mix to give power and further control a person. One can see how there is no escape from such a predicament save through the divine intervention of Jesus Christ working through the prayer and love of a committed Christian minister.

CHAPTER SIX

The Waters Become a River

Afterward he measured a thousand; and it was a river that I could not pass over: for the waters were risen, waters to swim in, a river that could not be passed over (Ezekiel 47:5).

Since that night when the presence of the Lord came to me and awakened my spiritual body, I have had the feeling of this gentle wave-like motion throughout my whole body. Floating down a gentle river would be a good analogy of what I am feeling. I know I am in the river of God's presence and He is continually bringing me closer and closer to a fuller manifestation of Himself. He is in the river with me. I know this not only by faith but by the feeling of His presence that never leaves. However, I don't hear His audible voice. He speaks to me in other ways that will be explained later. I see His face only in my imagination. That has become clearer over the past fifteen years of using my imagination to see Him, but I don't see Him as clearly as I see earthly things with my natural eyes.

Rivers are often used as boundaries between territories, states or nations with one bank of the river being in one territory and the opposite bank in the other territory; and so it is with this river. Our earthly existence and life as we have always known it is on one side, and heaven is on the other.

I mentioned previously that Jesus said to Nathanael in John One, "...ye shall see heaven open, and the angels of God ascending and descending upon the Son of man." Jesus is the One who bridges the gap between heaven and earth. He is the One Jacob saw as the ladder in Genesis 28:12, "...behold a ladder set upon the earth and the top of it reached to heaven: and behold the angels of God ascending and descending on it." Later Jacob proclaimed, "...this is the gate of heaven." Jesus said in John 10, "I am the door." It is only through Christ we are able to enter into the things of heaven in these last days. He is the gate. He is the door. He is the ladder, and He is the river.

Before the waters became a river, they were indistinct. There was a trickle here and a trickle there but not the defining force of a river. Now the person becomes aware of swimming or living between two distinct sides. He can see earth on one side, but he is now able to see heaven on the other side. Something has been awakened in him and he now has the capacity to see both sides at once. When this happens, he becomes aware that he can be in a group of people chatting about the weather and at the same time be worshiping God internally. There are now two sides to his being of which he is fully aware. It is as though one foot is on earth on one side of the river and the other foot is in heaven on the opposite side. This awareness of having two sides follows him wherever he goes. He can be sitting in a stadium watching a football game while feeling God's presence and worshiping Him at the same time.

This is a river that "could not be passed over," in the sense that it is not time for this person to leave his physical body and enter into heaven fully as one who has died. He does not fully pass to the other side leaving the earthly side behind but remains in the river with access to either side at once.

The River of Evil

The darkness of occult evil is sweeping over our nation like a flood, engulfing the hearts and minds of untold millions. Children's toys, books, cartoons and movies are increasingly centered in occult themes of witchcraft, wizardry, supernatural manifestations and powers. Horoscopes, signs of the Zodiac, psychic hotlines and satanic movies are becoming more popular as adults fall deeper into the enemy's deceptions. This river of wickedness and deceit flowing from the serpent's mouth is also a boundary between two territories—earth on one side and hell on the other. As people swim in this river, the rapids overtake them and cast them upon the banks of hell.

The flood of evil flowing from the serpent's mouth is totally opposite of God's river. God's river is smooth and clear as crystal bringing life and healing to everything it touches, but the evil one's flood is rough, murky and filled with sewage, debris, disease and death. It forces its way unwanted into homes, businesses and lands destroying everything in its path. Only those whose lives are hidden in Christ can escape the deception of this filthy river.

We must remember God is in control and "When the enemy shall come in like a flood, the Spirit of the Lord shall lift up a standard against him" (Isa. 59:19). The great flood of Noah's day destroyed all the wicked from the face of the earth, but Noah's family was safe in the ark. As we abide in our Ark, the Lord Jesus Christ, we too shall be safe. Noah's ark was lifted up by the floodwaters and eventually came to rest on the top of Mt. Ararat on the seventeenth day of the seventh month. This time corresponds to the Feast of Tabernacles that was to be instituted by God through Moses at a later date. I briefly touched on this feast earlier when I viewed it as a symbol of coming into the rest of God and into the fullness of His Spirit. As we, the Church, face this flood of evil, we must stand in the grace, love and power of the Lord Jesus Christ so we too will be lifted up to a high mountain, Mt. Zion, where we will find that all the evil in us has been destroyed. When the church comes into the fullness God has prepared for her, then the flood of evil will be destroyed as multitudes see the glory of God in His people and turn from their wicked ways.

Ministering to the satanically ritually abused opens our eyes to see and understand the wickedness of our enemy. Most Christians have no concept of evil beyond what they see with their natural eyes. The evil of SRA is incomprehensible but as we minister to its survivors and stand against the demons, we will find ourselves and those to whom we minister, being lifted up into new heights in Jesus Christ.

'Abar

We need to take another look at verses three through five of our text to examine the Hebrew word, 'abar, that appears several times in these three verses. I have put the English words translated from 'abar, in italics so we can see where this word appears.

> 3 And when the man that had the line in his hand went forth eastward, he measured a thousand cubits, and he *brought* me *through* the waters; the waters were to the ankles.
>
> 4 Again he measured a thousand, and *brought* me *through* the waters; the waters were to the knees. Again he measured a thousand, and *brought* me *through*; the waters were to the loins.
>
> 5 Afterward he measured a thousand; and it was a river that I could not *pass over*: for the waters were risen, waters to swim in, a river that could not be *passed over*."

As previously stated, this river typifies Christ as the One who bridges the gap between earth and heaven. When we think of earth and heaven, we think of them as being "out there," but we must remember this revelation is about what is taking place within the believer. This river is the revelation of Jesus Christ pouring forth from His Spirit to our spirit and into the rest of our being. Other Hebrew words for "brought" have been used in previous verses and will be in succeeding verses, but in this passage where the individual is going through the waters to the ankles, knees, loins, etc., the word, 'abar, is used exclusively.

'Abar means "to cross over," "transition," and "to cover (in copulation)." In this vision the person is transitioning, or crossing over, from an earthly, natural existence to a supernatural, heavenly one. In order for this to be accomplished, certain changes are taking place within him as the Holy Spirit works within. The Lord comes upon him and covers him as Elijah and Elisha each came upon a dead child, stretching over him that the Spirit of Life might be imparted to him. As Jesus Christ covers the believer, as His Spirit is imparted in ever increasing amounts, the two are becoming one fulfilling Jesus' prayer of John 17:23, "I in them, and thou in me, that they may be made perfect in one..."

Is this not what takes place in a marriage between husband and wife? Paul said in Ephesians 5:31,32, "For this cause shall a man leave his father and mother, and shall be joined unto his wife, and they two shall be one flesh. This is a great mystery: but I speak concerning Christ and the church." I am not suggesting anything sexual here between the Lord and His bride, the Church, but the type is clear. The oneness we experience in marriage on earth is but a type of the joining or becoming one of Christ and the Church.

Each time a husband and wife come together in the physical union of their marriage, they are, in effect, prophesying the coming together of Christ and His church in the Sabbath day. No wonder the Devil has so perverted and twisted the whole concept of sexuality until many have come to view it as something "dirty." The enemy has distorted, twisted and perverted human sexuality in every conceivable way so as to malign and somehow ruin the biblical type for the most wonderful event to take place in the history of mankind—the coming together of Christ and His Church, the joining of heaven and earth in the believer, resulting in the lifting of the curse from all aspects of humanity.

The Holy Spirit imparts ever-deepening revelations of Jesus Christ as this person dies to carnality (ankles) and enters into new depths of worship and adoration (knees). As the imagination is activated and unused portions of the brain begin to be awakened (loins), there comes a depth of understanding and experience that is immeasurable and limitless—enough to swim in!

This Hebrew word for "swim," *sachuw*, comes from the root, *sachah*, meaning "to inundate." This English word, "inundate," means "to move in waves," "to cover or engulf with a flood." How exciting it is for me to see the description of what I have been feeling for many years being described here in the Hebrew. "To move in waves" is exactly what I feel at all times. I look forward to the day when many others will have this experience. I believe something catastrophic is coming very soon and when it hits, God's presence as I have described it will be felt by true believers all over the world. This will bring great comfort and hope to all who love the Lord. They will know He is with them no matter what they are experiencing during this great crisis. They will know He has come to them personally in a way reserved for the Church of the end times.

The love of God is so deep, so unfathomable that we are incapable of understanding it and if we were to feel the magnitude of it all at once, we could not bear it. I have felt God's love at times so strongly I wondered if I could survive should He increase it even a tiny amount. His love is incredibly sweet, tender and gentle, yet at the same time so powerful I was aware He could crush me like an ant in an instant if He chose to do so. Of course, He would never do such a thing because He is love through and through, but the sense of His enormous power is awesome beyond words.

At this stage of the believer's experience, the love of God begins to sweep over him in waves of such enormity it is as though every cell of the body feels loved. God is awakening new aspects of the believer's being that hitherto have been dormant but are now being awakened to receive and experience these new depths of love. Oh! The joy and the peace that awaits the believer in these last days who is willing to cast aside all idolatrous loves and seek only pure devotion to Christ!

'Abar, Passing Through the Fire

This Hebrew word, *'abar*, also means "to pass through" and is translated thusly eleven times in Scripture concerning the practice of making children "pass through the fire" unto some god—usually Molech. It is listed along with other occult practices in Deuteronomy 18:10-12, "There shall not be found among you any one that maketh his son or his daughter to pass through the fire, or that useth divination, or an observer of times, or an enchanter, or a witch, or a charmer, or a consulter with familiar spirits, or a wizard, or a necromancer. For all that do these things are an abomination unto the Lord."

The enemies of Israel participated in these abominations and because the Hebrews mingled with these nations against God's commands, they too began to indulge in these evil practices. "Passing through the fire" refers to human sacrifice and is found in a list of sins including wizardry, for which sin Harry Potter is highly exalted amongst the young and spiritually uninformed of this nation and the world. It is true that children are still sacrificed to Satan in the fires of satanic rituals here and abroad, but far more children have been sacrificed through abortion on the altar of convenience.

It is interesting that the words "to pass through the fire" occur eleven times in Scripture because eleven is the number of disorder, disorganization, imperfection and disintegration. Perhaps this is one reason why our enemies chose September 11 as the date for their destructive attacks on the United States.

"Passing through the fire" not only pertains to human sacrifice, but also may refer to the cult practice of walking on hot coals. Sometimes SRA children are forced to walk barefooted over hot coals as a demonstration of their satanic powers. It is a common practice to demonstrate the child's powers in front of visiting cult authorities who, if impressed, will pay money for the "privilege" of raping her for her powers as the evil spirits are passed from her to them via sexual intercourse.

We need to understand that the wicked practices of satanic rituals are now coming out in the open and into the workplace in America. An article by Dave Barry in the Rochester Democrat and Chronicle of Monday, Nov.5, 2001 states that fire walking is considered to be a motivational tool to improve worker performance and increase sales:

> Fire walking was a planned activity on a corporate motivational retreat, supervised by a professional fire walking consultant to whom Burger King paid thousands of actual U.S. dollars. The consultant also had Burger King marketing people bend spoons, break boards, smash bricks, bend steel bars with their throats and walk over a bed of sharp nails. American corporate employees are required to do this kind of thing all the time...

These activities are only possible through utilization of satanic powers even though the person involved may not realize this.

We have seen that *'abar* also means "to cover (in copulation)." Sex, or copulation, is an important part of satanic rituals for several reasons—the most important reason would seem to be that of desecrating the most holy of all Christian relationships—marriage. Not only is marriage the highest form of relationship known on earth, but also it is a type of Christ and the Church (Eph. 5:32). Christ is coming for a pure, chaste Bride and the Devil is doing everything he can to ruin the whole concept of married love.

As stated earlier, another reason sexual intercourse is done in rituals is for the purpose of transferring demon spirits from person to person. Demon powers are put into the SRA child through the rituals. Those desiring her powers must rape her to access them. Every kind of sexual perversion known to man takes place at the rituals as a way of demonstrating total rebellion to God and His commandments.

'Abar means "to cross over," "transition," or "to cover (in copulation)." There seems to be something about sexual intercourse in most if not all societies that has to do with "crossing over" or "transition." Before the experience of sex, one is said to be a virgin, naïve, innocent, undefiled

and unknowing. After sex, one is deemed to have "crossed over" into adulthood or "transitioned" to a new era of life. To the cult mind, therefore, sexual intercourse is connected to crossing over to a new realm of rebellion against God and spiritual power. To rape a child or a virgin is to defile innocence and defy God—two things the Devil loves to do.

Even as believers become one with Christ and experience waves of His loving presence sweeping over them, those who have rejected God will be subjected to intense suffering as described in Revelation:

> *And the fifth angel sounded, and I saw a star fall from heaven unto the earth: and to him was given the key of the bottomless pit. And he opened the bottomless pit; and there arose a smoke out of the pit, as the smoke of a great furnace; and the sun and the air were darkened by reason of the smoke of the pit. And there came out of the smoke locusts upon the earth: and unto them was given power, as the scorpions of the earth have power. And it was commanded them that they should not hurt the grass of the earth, neither any green thing, neither any tree; but only those men which have not the seal of God in their foreheads. And to them it was given that they should not kill them, but that they should be tormented five months: and their torment was as the torment of a scorpion, when he striketh a man. And in those days shall men seek death, and shall not find it; and shall desire to die, and death shall flee from them (Rev. 9:1-6).*

Son of Man

> *And he said unto me, Son of man, hast thou seen this? Then he brought me, and caused me to return to the brink of the river (Ezekiel 47:6).*

This "crossing over" and "transitioning" from a mere earthly existence to a heavenly one while on earth will be accomplished as Jesus and the individual become one resulting in a total fulfillment of Galatians 2:20, "I am crucified with Christ: nevertheless I live; yet not I but Christ liveth in me..." At this juncture the person will be so totally yielded to Christ that Jesus will be able to do all things through him, even as promised in John 14:12, "He that believeth, the works that I do shall he do also; and greater works than these shall he do..."

Throughout the book of Ezekiel, the Lord has called him "Son of man" no less than 93 times, thereby giving Ezekiel the same name He used of Himself in the Gospels. I believe this in an indicator that there are many things in the book of Ezekiel that are especially pertinent to the Church of the end times. Here in this sixth verse of chapter 47, we find this name used for the last time.

As believers are perfected in the end time, the head, Jesus Christ, will be joined with a perfected body as the many-membered Body of Christ manifested in the earth. What a triumph over the Devil's feeble attempts to destroy Jesus Christ! He killed one physical body on the cross only to see it resurrected in power and glory; and as if that weren't enough, Jesus is now filling multitudes of last days' believers with Himself resulting in a many-membered body going every place on the earth doing the works Jesus did and even greater works! (This is not to say we will be God, but our character will be perfected so that whatever ministry God does through us will not be corrupted or misused.)

We will be brought to the place where the carnal self-will is dead and God will be able to manifest His power through us knowing that we will not be corrupted by it. Now the words, "in my name," connected with the New Testament promises, "if you ask anything," will come to fruition. Many times we believers have asked or commanded things from God tacking on the words, "in Jesus' name," as though those words were a formula for getting God to do something. The power of God has never been in saying certain words but in the yielded life of the one speaking those words.

Now that this life is being perfected and filled with Christ, the following promises of Scripture will be fulfilled in this person: "And whatsoever ye shall ask in my name, that will I do, that the Father may be glorified in the Son. If ye shall ask any thing in my name, I will do it (John 14:13,14). "Verily, verily, I say unto you, Whatsoever ye shall ask the Father in my name, he will give it you" (John 16:23).

(What is seen in the river chronologically may be happening in the believer simultaneously; therefore, as each experience of regeneration is explained, the individual will be said to be perfected even though more of the process of being perfected is yet to be seen in the following verses.)

In this sixth verse of Ezekiel 47, after Jesus calls him, "Son of man," for the last time, He asked a question, "have you seen this?" He is really asking, "Do you 'understand' this?" knowing that this person has not yet fully comprehended what has taken place in him spiritually nor the magnitude of the life that now fills him.

Sons of Man or Sons of Satan

As believers come into the fullness of Christ and become like Him in their character and ministries, Satanists will take on the very nature of Satan himself. We are going to experience the fullness of good and the fullness of evil clashing head-on in the days ahead and, most assuredly, good will ultimately triumph over evil. However, there will be a lot of suffering.

In order for the Church to come into full maturity, she must learn to stand against the fullness of evil. The principle seen here in the spiritual realm is also seen in the physical. The only way to have strong muscles is to exercise them by resisting the force or weight brought against them. Astronauts living in the weightlessness of space have to recondition their muscles upon their return to earth because, in the absence of the earth's gravitational pull, their muscles begin to atrophy. When we stand against evil, we exercise our spiritual "muscles" and thereby grow into full maturity. The evil that Satan intends for destruction only works for our good and God's ultimate purpose when we respond according to God's commands.

Evil men in power who experience the torment of demons will be driven to commit increasingly greater acts of wickedness in their attempts to alleviate the suffering of their tormented souls and bodies. They will be like the wicked described in Pr. 4:16, "For they sleep not, except they have done mischief; and their sleep is taken away, unless they cause some to fall." Some readers may remember the tragic serial killer nicknamed "Son of Sam." There were times when he could not sleep until he had committed a murder.

God will have a place of safety for those who truly love Him as seen symbolically in Rev. 12:6, 15, 16, "And the woman fled into the wilderness, where she hath a place prepared of God…And the serpent cast out of his mouth water as a flood after the woman, that he might cause her to be carried away of the flood. And the earth helped the woman, and the earth opened her mouth, and swallowed up the flood which the dragon cast out of his mouth."

The Brink of the River

Jesus expands his vision further as verse six continues, "Then he brought me, and caused me to return to the brink of the river."

An examination of the Hebrew words for "brought," *yalak*, and "return," *shuwb*, in *Gesenius' Hebrew-Chaldee Lexicon*, reveal that Jesus "brought him," *yalak*, and caused him to "turn back, not to where he had been before, but to a place he had never been," *schuwb*.

In the definition for the Hebrew word "brink," *saphah*, we find the following: "through the idea of termination," "to open the lips for speech," "language," and "side."

I'm going to tie these words and their definitions together into a spiritual interpretation that will further expand our understanding of the process we will go through as we go down this river unto perfection. I'm going to begin with the definitions for "brink" that mean "to open the lips for speech" and "language."

First of all, we know that we can never enter into this new life of perfection by our own efforts. Only God can bring us here. However, we will need to cooperate with God so He can do what He desires in our lives. This will require a new dimension of communication with God. Relationship with God is essential if we are to rise up in maturity in Him, and good relationships require good communication.

Many years ago, back in the mid '70s, I decided that my prayer life was too much of a monologue. I wanted communication with God to be a two-way thing. The Holy Spirit gave me an idea of how to hear from God. (I didn't know it was the Holy Spirit at the time, but I knew it enabled me to hear God, so it had to have been from Him.) Here is how it worked. I would pray for awhile and then ask God to speak to me by giving me chapter and verse from the Bible. I would look up whatever came into my head not having any idea what that scripture verse would say. It was amazing how clearly I learned to hear from God using this "method." I would always write down in a spiral notebook God's answers to my prayers. I still have those old notebooks along with many more accumulated over the years.

This only worked when I had prayed earnestly for a period of time. We can never use God just to get what we want or manipulate Him. I used to pray for at least a half hour sometimes an hour...long enough to really be in communication with Him...and then He was faithful to answer. Sometimes I would ask, "Do you have anything to say to me?" and the scripture I would be given tied in perfectly with something I had been praying about.

Here is one example of how amazing this way of communication really was. I had been ministering for satanic ritual abuse for two or three years when I decided that I needed to get a master of counseling degree. I completed my first course and was getting ready to sign up for the second when I began to feel a heavy burden about it. I didn't know what to do.

Early one morning I began to earnestly seek God about my situation. I poured out my heart to Him about the whole thing. Then I asked Him to give me chapter and verse regarding what He wanted me to do. The thought came into my mind to read Ecclesiastes 12:12, 13. After turning to that passage, here is what I read,

And further, by these, my son, be admonished: of making many books there is no end; and much study is a weariness of the flesh. Let us hear the conclusion of the whole matter: Fear God, and keep his commandments: for this is the whole duty of man.

God's message was clear. All the study I would have to do would be wearisome. There is no end to the books I could read on the subject. The most important thing was that I stay in close relationship with God and walk in obedience to Him.

I had not been reading Ecclesiastes. This came into my head straight from the Holy Spirit. It was to be a few years before I understood why I was not to take these courses. God wanted me to succeed in this ministry by following His direction and leaning entirely upon His Holy Spirit. If I had taken courses, I would have started following someone's counseling technique instead of listening to the Holy Spirit. Also, He wanted me to be an example to others in the church that all is required to successfully minister for SRA is that we be called of God.

I enjoyed many wonderful words from God over a period of several years using this way of hearing, but one day it all came to an end. Here is where anther word for the definition of "brink" comes into play. "Brink" in Hebrew not only means "language" but also "termination." The way I was used to hearing from God came to an end. However, God did not leave me without a way of hearing His voice. He just began to speak in another way that was far higher and better than what I had enjoyed for so many years. This leads us to the other Hebrew words, *yalak* and *shuwb*.

Jesus brought me (*yalak*) back to hearing from Him again but not to where I had been before (*shuwb*). I began to hear from Him in a different way. This way of hearing was totally new to me. I had never heard anyone speak of hearing Him in this way. It all started when my spiritual body was awakened.

Shortly after my spiritual body had been awakened I became aware of Jesus communicating with me through feeling in my body. The first word I learned to hear was "yes." This might sound very limited, but actually there have been many personal and detailed messages coming to me just by His saying "yes." I know I'm hearing "yes" when my face feels warm as though the sun were shining on it.

By way of example I want to share what I recently experienced where God's word "yes" spoke volumes to me. I went through a trial involving a chronic tooth abscess of which I had not been aware. To make a very long story short, I had a root canal and then a crown put on the tooth. Immediately after the crown was put on, I had terrible pain that persisted with no relief. I was on the Internet reading a site about root canals that said root canals are not good and should be removed. When I read that, I felt that warmth on my face. I said, "Lord, are You telling me this tooth has to be pulled?" Then another wave of warmth came over me. As I talked with the Lord, these waves kept coming. I knew beyond the shadow of a doubt that God was saying to have that tooth pulled even though I had just spent about $2,500 on it.

The next day I called my dentist and asked to see him as soon as possible. Being the great guy that he is, he told me to come right in. He is a Christian man so I was able to tell him that God told me to have him pull the tooth even though he had just put a crown on it. He had me sign a statement that he was pulling it per my request since there was nothing on the x-ray to show anything wrong. Then he pulled the tooth, and lo and behold, under it was gutta percha from a botched root canal (that he did not do) and many granules that had formed over the years of that chronic abscess. He was astounded at all the stuff he found under the tooth that had never showed on the x-ray

I thought that would take care of the pain, but the pain persisted for two or more weeks. My jaw felt swollen. I knew something was wrong. I was thinking, maybe I need to see an oral surgeon. Then the warmth came on my face again. I was to feel it strongly twice that morning as I was praying and determining what to do.

Again I called my dentist; he made the appointment with the oral surgeon even though he didn't think I needed one. She operated on the extraction site and found many more granules underneath the site that could only have been removed through surgery. Then I got well, although it has seemed to take a very long time, cost more money and, as of the writing of this book, I still don't have a tooth there.

So you can see that just the word "yes" from God can be of tremendous value. When I am thinking something and then I feel that warmth, I know for certain that God is saying "yes." God has spoken this word to me countless times, often it is not about something really important, but He is teaching me that when He says "yes" in conjunction with what I am thinking, He is right without fail. I may be looking for something (I seem to do that a lot) and when I feel that warmth, I know I'll find what I'm looking for if I persist.

This is just one of the communications I get from Him through feeling. A pain in my body can be a warning. One time I was walking up the steep road near our home when I suddenly experienced a sharp pain in my groin. I thought, "This is ridiculous; I walk up this hill almost every day." The pain was so severe, I was not able to continue going up the hill. As soon as I turned back down, the pain left. I walked up other steep hills on our property that day without pain. It was clearly a warning not to walk up that road alone. That night I had a dream. In my dream, I was walking up that same road when a car stopped and abducted me. I found myself a prisoner in some strange city with no way to get home. I know now that I am only to walk up that road if my husband is with me. It is not safe to go alone even though we live in the country and know most of our neighbors. I also know that whenever I am headed in a dangerous direction, God will warn me.

These are just two of many ways I hear God through my body. Many things I feel from Him have to do with His constant nearness to me and His love. All believers are going to need to feel these things as our way of life is threatened and evil seems to abound on all sides. God is with us and He can see us through whatever comes if we will cling to Him and trust Him rather than our own understanding. It is much easier to do this when we are actually feeling his presence in our body.

A Different Side

Part of the definition for "brink," *saphah*, means "side." The word "side" will also be seen in the next verse of this Ezekiel passage where trees are visible on either side of the river. Throughout this book I have been writing about a side of our being of which we have been unaware that God will be awakening in these end times. I have been able to hear God in this new way because a side of my being of which I have been unaware has been awakened by God. This spiritual side of my being consists of a spiritual body and a spiritual mind. As my spiritual body has been awakened I have become aware of having a spiritual mind also. Most of my awareness of the opening of my spiritual mind has been through revelation in the Scriptures. I feel that I am in the infancy stages regarding this new side of my being. I know God is in charge and He determines this whole process as I participate with Him by hearing and obeying.

At this point I would like to insert an excerpt from an article I wrote for my website a few years ago that will reinforce some of the things I have been relating here along with giving more details about our spiritual mind.

The Spiritual Mind and the Wheel within a Wheel

A common memory for a woman who was satanically ritually abused is one of having given birth to a baby who was tortured and sacrificed to Satan. Such a memory is painful and terrifying beyond anything imaginable. After such a memory, I ask Jesus to minister to her. As He ministers to her, she is able to see and hear Him. He lets her see her baby and even hold the baby in her arms for a minute right in my office in front of me. I can't see or hear any of the things she is experiencing.

My question for years was why can't I see and hear also? From the very beginning of the SRA ministry twenty years ago, I noticed that the survivor, the demons, Jesus—everyone connected with a ministry situation could see what was going on but me. I always wondered why I couldn't. After many years of study, I have found some interesting answers in God's Word.

As we turn to the Bible, God will reveal why most of us do not see into the spiritual realm yet and at the same time He will reveal why we may be able to do so in the future.

There is more than one reason we cannot experience this realm. The reason I want to bring forth here concerns the human mind and the abilities of the mind that were lost as a result of Adam and Eve's disobedience that plunged us all into the fall. Adam had the ability to hear God's voice as He walked in the garden. He was able also to name all the cattle, birds and beasts the Lord God brought before him, a task of gargantuan proportions. Clearly he had mental abilities we do not have. A look at the four living creatures of Ezekiel One will help us understand more about why Adam had these abilities and we do not.

My studies have revealed that the four living creatures are representative of mature Christians (not literally only four; four represents man in relation to the earth as created) who will minister in great power at the end of this age. Ezekiel One reveals their preparation for this incredible ministry and Chapter Ten describes their ministry. This ministry will astound the world and prepare the way for Christ's millennial reign upon the earth. (See my book entitled, *The Four Living Creatures*.)

Anyone who has read about these four living creatures probably remembers they had a wheel within a wheel. We will delve into the mystery of the wheels in a moment, but first I want to explain that these chapters about the four living creatures were written in such a way that only God could reveal their hidden meaning. It was written in this way because they contain information God intended for use only by the great Church of the end times—information that will prepare us to meet our Bridegroom as the Holy Spirit works in us to bring us to the condition of having neither spot nor wrinkle.

Demons, having spiritual abilities and intelligence far above that of human beings, know some of the secrets contained in these encoded passages of Scripture. They have perverted and used this information to deceive human beings and entice them into a realm of spirit that God lovingly closed to us after the fall. As previously stated, God knew that we can only see spiritually according to what is in our own heart because truth is always seen from the heart not the intellect. Since none of us is perfected yet, we all have darkness in our heart. This means that should we be able to hear and see into the spirit realm, we would be deceived and/or terrorized by the demons, which is exactly what has happened to persons subjected to satanic ritual abuse. As we delve into a few passages of Scripture, we will see that SRA has propelled persons into a dimension of spirit God closed to us for our own protection way back in the Garden of Eden. Some of this has to do with the wheel within the wheel.

The Scriptures will reveal that the wheel in these passages is the mind. The Hebrew definition for wheel, *'owphan,* means, "to revolve." In the New Testament Paul says to Timothy, "Meditate on these things" (1 Tim 4:15). This word "meditate" in Greek is *meletao* and means "to revolve in the mind" and "imagine."

A wheel revolves. We allow something to revolve in our mind when we meditate. We go over and over something in our mind— round and round we mentally go as we fret over something, relive an experience, try to solve a problem, etc.

The Word tells us, "Let this mind be in you, which was also in Christ Jesus" (Phil. 2:5) and "...we have the mind of Christ" (1 Cor. 2:16). This is the wheel within the wheel—the human mind and the mind of Christ within a Christian.

Knowing that the wheels refer to the mind of Christ within our mind, this next verse becomes very revelatory, "for the spirit of the living creature was in the wheels" (Ezekiel 1:20 and 1:21). This fact is so important it is stated twice in these two verses. Our spirit is within our mind! (Eph. 4:23 tells us to "be renewed in the spirit of your mind.) This information is mind-boggling. It begins to reveal something of the vastness of the human mind because spirit is without limit. The human mind also contains our imagination, long understood by cults as being the way to access the realm of spirit.

From this information we can deduce that the realm of spirit that is closed to us is entered via the human mind because the spirit is within the mind. However, we cannot will ourselves to enter into this realm of spirit. The veils that close off this part of our mind have to be removed either by God as we are perfected or by demons accessed through occult activities. The activation of the spiritual realm should be done only as our character is purified, and all of this is determined by God.

As we think about the vast capabilities of the human mind that reside in the unused part of our mind and that the spirit is within the mind, we can begin to understand more about the spiritual phenomena we see in SRA—astral projection for example. The mind doesn't leave the body and neither does the spirit. This is all transpiring within the human mind, part of our being that is more spiritual and comprehensive than we have ever perceived but still attached to our physical body.

Another application for SRA is in regards to the alternate personality parts formed during the extreme distress of satanic rituals. Are some of these alters trapped in dimensions outside of the body as some are teaching? No, they are all parts of the person's personality that have split off from the main stream of consciousness. Our personality does not leave our body, even though it has been split into sometimes numerous parts. Demons have power to deceive all of us. We must be very careful to let the Bible guide our understanding as we try to understand the bizarre things we encounter in SRA ministry. The answers are usually beneath the surface of the Word so we must pray and search diligently. As we do so, the Holy Spirit will guide us into all truth.

The 19th-century author, Andrew Jukes, writes of the vastness of the inner life in his book, *Types in Genesis*. Referring to Genesis and the forms of life that spring out of Adam, Jukes writes:

> For the development of Adam or human nature in the great world without, has its exact image and counterpart in the little world within; I call it 'little,' though indeed it is not little; for if 'the kingdom of God is within us,' there must be room enough. And what confusion it seems: life and death, evil and good, love and hate, and pride and meanness everywhere: men praying, cursing, blessing; palaces and hovels, churches and armies, schools and markets, jails, cities, asylums, unions; such are some of the fruits of old Adam, in whom all this was before it was seen, and is only seen without because it was and is within him. (Jukes 1993, xv)

We know that we only use a small part of our mind. During satanic rituals, demons begin awakening the dormant parts of the mind as they remove partitions or veils placed there by God to shield us from the spiritual realm. As these partitions are removed, areas of the mind are awakened that enable persons to see and hear demons. This is, of course, a terrifying experience especially for a child.

In my estimation, satanic ritual abuse is the most horrific experience any human being could endure. It just doesn't get any worse! However, this is all going to backfire on the enemy and result in all his plans for ruling the world and enslaving humanity being foiled.

We know the Devil cannot create anything. He can only counterfeit that which God has made. God made everything for good. The realm of spirit that has been entered through satanic rituals was intended for the Church of the end times. We will enter according to the goodness in our heart and, therefore, will experience the good side of this realm. As we become the Church without spot or wrinkle, as we come into the measure of the stature of the fullness of Christ, God wants to righteously take us into new realms of spirit.

Our minds were shut up because of the fall—because of sin. As God removes the sin in us through our identification with his death and resurrection, as we deny ourselves, take up our cross daily and follow Him and come into end-time perfection, He will remove the partitions in our mind and take us into new spiritual depths in Him. Without a doubt, this is something only God can do, and it will be done only as the Church rises to a place in Him never before attained by any Christian of any generation.

When God takes us into new realms of spiritual experience in Him, we will see Him face to face, we will hear the glorious music and voices of heaven, and we will minister in the fullness of the Holy Spirit in ways that will astound the world. We read in 1 John 3, "Beloved, now are we the sons of God, and it doth not yet appear what we shall be: but we know that, when he shall appear, we shall be like him; for we shall see him as he is. And every man that hath this hope in him purifieth himself, even as he is pure." I'm not there yet, but I know I'm on my way.

The following is an account of an experience I had in 1986 that demonstrates that at some point we will enter into a new realm of spirit. I had just started ministering to persons who had suffered satanic ritual abuse. I was totally baffled by what I saw and prayed to see and hear more spiritual things. I was totally ignorant about the ramifications of what I was asking, but God in His great mercy did not let me see these things knowing I would have been destroyed by the experience.

We lived on 200 acres of farmland and woods at the time. I used to walk around the property for hours praying and begging God to open my eyes to the spiritual realm so I could also see what was happening. After about two months of praying this way every day, a friend of mine invited me to a women's meeting at her church where a prophetess of the Lord was going to be ministering. I attended along with about fifty other women. At the end of the guest speaker's excellent teaching, she singled out about eight women for a prophetic message. I was one of those chosen. Here is some of what she said to me:

> In you God is stirring the gift of discerning of spirits and
> you're going to see that begin to come to perfection. You're
> going to know when angels are operating. You're going to know
> when God's Spirit is moving. You're going to know when the
> flesh is operating. You're going to know when demonic spirits
> are operating. You're going to see angels. You're going to see
> demonic forces. He is going to fulfill that in you and you are
> going to minister that gift out in the body of Christ.

Absolutely no one knew how I had been praying! This word was
definitely from God, and I was so excited! I expected to see spiritual
beings at my next ministry appointment. That was twenty-seven years
ago and I have yet to see anything (well, once about ten years ago
I saw a dark shadow quickly dart over the heads of a survivor and
myself after casting out a demon). Now I understand that this realm
of ministry will only come when I have reached that place of being
without spot or wrinkle. Until then, God can accomplish by His Spirit
all things needed to help the SRA persons He sends my way. To God
be the glory!

The Brink of the River—Evil Supernatural Communication

Many of those involved in satanic cults are highly skilled and
professionally trained in the areas of mind control, drugs and witchcraft,
all of which can be used for evil communication purposes. As Jesus
Christ is opening new avenues of supernatural communication for the
believer with Himself, Satanists are using demonic powers in order to
spy on and control others. In fact, they have been doing these things for
decades, if not longer. God has been waiting to open the supernatural
to His people until we die to self and come into maturity.

The satanically ritually abused are often controlled by personal,
supernatural messages delivered by the cult via demons and
programming. By means of deception, programming and drugs, the
satanically ritually abused are made to believe electronic devices such as

walky-talkies, radio receivers, tape recorders, etc. have been implanted in them through surgery. They actually hear instructions or tormenting shrieking sounds via this "equipment," but it is actually the demons they hear.

The cults, through rituals, can send demons into SRA persons from a great distance with detailed instructions for them to perform certain tasks or behaviors. The cult's power to control their victims is great, but the power of Jesus is greater and through prayer and deliverance, the programming can be removed and the demons cast out. Even apart from prayer and deliverance, God allows things to go only so far, and then He puts a stop to it. He is our sovereign Lord and He still reigns even though it might not look like it at times.

In contrast, God's people have the indwelling Holy Spirit to teach, counsel and guide them into all truth. All we have to do is love God and obey Him and come into the rest and peace He has for us. Satanists are deeply tormented people, unable to rest, who have to work very hard to devise their schemes for control to achieve their wicked ends.

Demons are able to implant their suggestions directly into the thoughts of those whose hearts and minds are not guarded by Christ Jesus. The SRA are programmed for abuse in many ways, one being the implantation of what I call "broadcasting" demons. These demons send out signals to demons in and around other people to activate the humans to say and do hurtful things to the abused person. These people don't realize what they are doing but are just being used by the enemy.

In my early days of SRA ministry, I used to wonder if people who consistently said hurtful things were part of the satanic cult, but over the years I've learned more about what is transpiring in the spiritual realm. The following illustration comes to mind.

One dear lady to whom I was ministering had gone through a dreadful memory of being shocked with cattle prods by her abusers. The next day, while still raw with the pain of the memory, she was with a group of church people who, for some strange reason, started talking about people being shocked with cattle prods. She almost went to pieces in front of them. As far as I know, these people had no idea about her abuse but had enough carnality in them to unknowingly act on a demonic suggestion. For the severely ritually abused, the road of life is full of boulders, shards of glass, deep pits and obstacles. Physical pain, emotional pain and curses plague them at every turn. It is a difficult walk, and they need our love, support and whenever possible, our protection.

CHAPTER SEVEN

The Trees by the River

Now when I had returned, behold, at the bank of the river were very many trees on the one side and on the other (Ezekiel 47:7).

After Jesus carries him and causes him to turn back, not to where he has been before, but to a place he has never been, his spiritual eyes are opened even more (behold) to see heavenly things. The trees he sees are all different aspects of the mature life of Christ now flourishing within himself. His union with Christ, death of the sin nature, a life of worship and adoration combined with the opening of the unused portions of the mind have brought him to a deeper revelation of Christ and of who he is in Christ.

This same river, as seen in Revelation 22, reveals these trees are indeed the tree of life, but here it has multiplied, each tree representing various characteristics of Christ that have come to maturity and fruition in the believer's life. As we read in Genesis 1:11, "Let the earth bring forth grass, the herb yielding seed, and the fruit tree yielding fruit after his kind..." so is the progression of the life of a believer. We begin in the flesh, "For all flesh is as grass, and all the glory of man as the flower of grass" (1 Peter 1:24). We progress into aromatic, flavorful herbs and finally fruit bearing trees (Matthew 13:32). The believer has come to maturity.

The fact that these trees are on one side and the other side of this river reveals that what had previously been possible only in heaven is now possible on earth, too, for both sides of the river are now the same. This person no longer has a two-sided nature with one side being spiritual and the other carnal. Now both sides of his being are perfected and filled with the fruitfulness of Jesus' very life. He has come to the place where Jesus' prayer of John 17 is fulfilled, "And the glory which thou gavest me I have given them; that they may be one, even as we are one: I in them, and thou in me, that they may be made perfect in one..."

At this point in the believer's life, all the promises of Scripture are fulfilled in him and there is no longer any hindrance to the full manifestation of the life of Christ in him. He has come unto the "... knowledge of the Son of God, unto a perfect man, unto the measure of the stature of the fullness of Christ" (Ephesians 4:13).

The Corrupt Trees by the River

Trees are symbolic of fruitfulness. Jesus, in speaking of false prophets, warned us to judge them by their fruits.

> *Beware of false prophets, which come to you in sheep's clothing, but inwardly they are ravening wolves. Ye shall know them by their fruits. Do men gather grapes of thorns, or figs of thistles? Even so every good tree bringeth forth good fruit; but a corrupt tree bringeth forth evil fruit. A good tree cannot bring forth evil fruit, neither can a corrupt tree bring forth good fruit. Every tree that bringeth not forth good fruit is hewn down, and cast into the fire. Wherefore by their fruits ye shall know them (Matt. 7:15-20).*

This is an extremely important caution for the day in which we live as evil is coming over our earth in many forms, and God has warned us saying, "For there shall arise false Christs, and false prophets, and shall show great signs and wonders; insomuch that, if it were possible, they shall deceive the very elect" (Matt. 24:24). There is a tendency amongst some Christians to judge every supernatural manifestation as being of God. We must be prayerful and discerning of whether or not to follow certain religious leaders. We must not make the mistake of believing numbers of people represent fruitfulness. A ministry is valid when we see the character of Jesus in the minister, the pure Word of God preached and maturity in the lives of those under him. Miraculous healings, prophetic words, or people falling down "in the Spirit" are not to be seen as fruit because the Devil can do all these things, and will do them, to get people to follow a deceiver. Deceivers will lead people straight into the acceptance of a one-world religion. We see an emphasis for this with media pressure to accept Islam as a viable religion on par with Christianity. Since the World Trade Center bombings there have been numerous prayer and worship services where Christians, Moslems and those of other faiths gathered "as one body."

A relative of mine who believes all religions lead to God, told me about the "wonderful" combined church services going on in her community where Christians, Muslims and Jews all gather together for monthly services. The messages are alternately delivered by a Christian minister, a rabbi or an imam. She told of one service that ran unusually long. The call for prayer sounded for the Muslims, who all immediately fell down on their prayer blankets bowing toward Mecca. The Christians, desiring to show their unity and acceptance of the Muslims, bowed down towards Mecca with them. I guess the Christians forgot about the three Hebrew youths in Daniel who preferred being cast into a fiery furnace to bowing down to an idol! Christians need to speak out about the fact that Jesus Christ and Allah are not the same God and Islam is not a religion of peace. Those who are not grounded in the Word of God are being misled.

We must pray for discernment. If one learns anything in the satanic ritual abuse ministry, it is that many things are not as they appear. You hear memory after memory about terrible atrocities and murders. Then you walk out into society and everyone seems so nice and you wonder, How can this be? Then you hear more memories and see the devastated lives and the manifestation of demons and you have to conclude, Yes, this is really happening. Ministering to the satanically ritually abused and living in our society requires an adjustment in our thinking. We must learn to minister to the oppressed, set the captives free and then leave it all behind and go on with our life. This takes maturity.

The East Country

Thus far in our study, we have seen the living waters flowing from the spirit into the area of the soul, the opening of the spiritual eyes to perceive the things of heaven and the presence of Jesus gradually coming to the believer. In verse eight, the healing waters begin flowing out into the physical body.

> *Then he said unto me, These waters issue out toward the east country, and go down into the desert, and go into the sea: which being brought forth into the sea, the waters shall be healed (Ezekiel 47:8).*

The Hebrew word for "said," *amar*, also means "commanded." The word for "issued out," *yatsa'* also means "sent with commandment," so we could just as well say that He (Jesus) commanded the healing waters to go forth to the east country.

As we shall see, the east country is the natural (physical) body. All through Scripture, judgment comes from the East. Our bodies have been under the judgment of death since Adam's fall in the garden. Our natural body is the country in which we live as revealed by the special word for "country" used in this passage.

Our English word, "country" or "countries" appears in the King James Version of the Old Testament 234 times. There are nine different Hebrew words that are translated "country." The word for country used here, *gelihlah*, is only used one time out of the 234 references. When something stands alone like this, it is as though the Holy Spirit is waving a flag over the word to catch our attention. There must be something very special about this word, *geliylah*, to have been selected for use in this passage. The only way to determine why this word was used is to examine the definitions of all nine Hebrew words for "country" to see why this one is different.

An examination of all these words reveals *gelihlah* is the only Hebrew word translated "country" that has "circuit" or "border" in its definition. A border goes around a country. Our word "circuit" is from the Latin, *circuitus* meaning "a going around." Our life is a circuit. Remember the old cliché, "You only go around once in life"? God says it in different words, "...for dust thou art, and unto dust shalt thou return" (Gen. 3:19). This is the state of the physical body—always progressing towards its inevitable end—death—and returning to the earth from which it was formed.

A border is a dividing line between two countries. Is not the physical body a border that keeps us divided from our heavenly country beyond the grave making us pilgrims and sojourners on this earth? A border confines us, places limitations upon us, even as a physical body, especially one aged or diseased, places boundaries and limitations upon us.

An examination of the word "country" in the New Testament also brings greater understanding to this passage. Out of seven Greek words translated "country," only one, *perichoros*, means "around the region" or "circumjacent." It is fascinating that in each of the two languages chosen by God for our Bible, there are multiple words for "country" but in each language only one word implies something being round or circuitous. This is highly significant.

There arc seven New Testament passages using this word, *perichoros*. Six of these passages are about physical healing and the seventh states Jesus was "glorified of all." In these passages they go into the "region round about" and bring all the sick people to Jesus for healing; or rumors about Jesus go into the "region round about" and the disciples of John come asking "Art thou he that should come? Or look we for another?" The answer is, "and in that same hour he cured many of their infirmities and plagues, and of evil spirits; and unto many that were blind he gave sight."

John the Baptist went into the "country round about" Jordan and preached saying, among other things, "All flesh shall see the salvation of God." Jesus is coming to our "region round about," our physical body, to heal us of all disease and sickness. For six days (6000 years) we have needed healing for our bodies, but in the seventh day (Sabbath day), the day we are beginning to enter, we will no longer need to be healed; we will only stand in our perfected bodies and glorify God for all He has done. All of our flesh will have experienced the full salvation and healing of God.

The East Country—the Physical Body and Satanic Powers

We know that God desires for His people to have healthy bodies and that sickness and disease come from the enemy. The more we are conformed to the image of Christ, the more strength and faith we have to resist any attack of the enemy on our body. However, Satan will sometimes "heal" someone in return for something he desires such as their allegiance to him. There are books, such as *The Beautiful Side of Evil* by Johanna Michaelson, that document satanic healings.

One of the evil powers of SRA persons may pertain to healing. One SRA woman told me about being summoned to her evil father's hospital bedside where he lay severely ill. When he reached out to her, she felt powers leave her body that seemed to strengthen him. That was the turning point in his illness and he recovered. This happened many years before she began having memories of her abuse and being delivered from all the demons.

I have heard many stories about strange healings that take place at satanic rituals but all these have been related to me by women who were severely traumatized at the ritual and vulnerable to trickery. It is not uncommon for someone ritually abused to believe their body was dismembered and then miraculously put back together again. This was probably done by the victim being traumatized, given drugs, and made to feel pain while being told a body part was cut off. Then a body part from some dead person was shown to her and she believed it was hers.

There does seem to be one supernatural type of healing that is commonly seen in the satanically ritually abused and that is freedom from scars. Scars that could validate their memories seem to be conspicuously absent. However, their internal organs, when exposed through surgery, often show tremendous inner scarring and damage that cannot be explained by physicians who know nothing about this kind of abuse.

Many people who have been satanically ritually abused suffer debilitating physical ailments as a result of their abuse. Some common illnesses seen in those so abused are migraine headaches, eating disorders (anorexia, bulimia, obesity, food addictions), sexual dysfunction, fibromyalgia, digestive tract problems (acid reflux, ulcers, colitis), blood chemistry imbalance, pain in joints of hips, heart problems, substance abuse, temporomandibular joint syndrome (TMJ), diseased reproductive organs, liver or adrenal malfunctions, thyroid disorder, arthritis or lupus, and many others.

The Desert

We have just observed the healing waters flowing out to the physical body (east country) and now we see them flowing into the desert.

Jesus said, "I have yet many things to say unto you, but ye cannot bear them now. Howbeit when he, the Spirit of truth, is come, he will guide you into all truth: for he shall not speak of himself; but whatsoever he shall hear, that shall he speak: and he will show you things to come" (John 16:12, 13). Our spiritual explanation for the desert will be one of those things Jesus could not speak about when He was on earth. It was not to be understood until the time of the end of the age.

As we examine the Hebrew word for "desert," *arabah*, we will find many clues leading us to believe this is referring to the spiritual body.

"There is a natural body, and there is a spiritual body" (1 Corinthians 15:44b). As stated earlier, until now our spiritual body has been something of which we have been unaware that was needed only when the physical body was vacated at the time of death. God will be awakening the spiritual body in one of the steps of bringing us into the fullness of Christ that "...when he shall appear, we shall be like him" (1 John 3:2b).

In times past we have interpreted this passage to mean we will be like Him spiritually only, but in these last days we will need to be like Him in every respect. We are going to need bodies that can survive chemical, biological and nuclear warfare. As the entire world is plunged into the darkness of the New World Order and the reign of the Antichrist, we will need a glorified body free from sin, one that knows no limitations. As God removes the seals from His Word, we will find many texts that describe the process we will experience as we are perfected.

There are six Hebrew words translated "desert," but the one used here, *arabah*, is distinctly different from all the others. The others mean "desolate," "solitary," "drought," "decayed," "lonesome," "waste place," etc., but *arabah* means "sterile," "evening," "heaven," with no mention of desolation or anything negative. As we shall see, an examination of each English definition for *arabah* will support the revelation that it represents the spiritual body.

A sterile desert brings to mind a place where nothing is growing or reproducing. There are no trees swaying in the wind or little animals scurrying around, no water—only lifeless sand as far as the eye can see. Our spiritual body has been that way in that we have felt nothing there—no movement. It has been as though it didn't exist—as though it wasn't alive—but once Jesus begins to awaken it, movement is felt there. A new revelation dawns upon us as we experience the awakening of a part of our being that has seemed nonexistent until this time. As the spiritual body awakens, the first thing we feel is "the touch of the Master's hand." It requires a spiritual body to feel a spiritual touch and with the awakening of this part of our being, we have a new capacity for experiencing Jesus' love even though we still have our physical body. Now our "desert shall rejoice, and blossom as the rose. It shall blossom abundantly, and rejoice even with joy and singing" (Isaiah 35).

Another aspect of the word "sterile" is in regard to medicine. Surgical instruments are sterilized to kill all the microorganisms living there. Where there are no harmful bacteria or viruses, most diseases are eliminated. A spiritual body is one that can never be attacked with sickness or infirmity of any kind because it is sterile in the sense that no microorganisms can grow there.

"Evening" speaks of the last part of the day or the last part of life. We are in the evening of this age, about to enter into a new age. It is obvious that man now has the power and the ability to destroy life on earth as we know it. As we experience the last days' harvest of all that is good and all that is evil, we are naïve if we think men walking in the fullness of evil will not use the weapons of mass destruction at their disposal. The time of God's judgment is upon us and we will have to be changed if we are to survive the great upheaval that is coming, but God has a plan for His people that includes more than survival—He desires to bring us into His fullness and open heaven before us.

The next word in our definition for "desert" is "heaven." If one has never been in a desert at night, it may be difficult to grasp this association. A desert is a place where there are no buildings, no city lights, no forests—nothing between heaven and earth—absolutely no barriers to obstruct one's view of heaven. There is only an immense display of brilliant, blazing stars and heavenly bodies from horizon to horizon seemingly close enough to reach up and touch. This speaks of the open heaven we will experience with the awakening of our spiritual body.

Jesus, the Father, the angels, and all the saints who have passed on before us are in a spiritual realm called "heaven." We do not presently see them, hear their voices or feel their touch because we are in physical bodies that relate only to a physical world. Once our spiritual bodies are awakened, we will be able to experience all of heaven. This commonly unknown truth about our spiritual bodies will help open our understanding of some difficult biblical passages. I would like to share one such passage from 1 Thessalonians 4:13-17. Keep in mind that not only do we have a spiritual body but also a spiritual mind that is said to be asleep or dead, and as these are awakened, we can experience a limitless, vast inner world as real, or more real, than our physical world. As you read the following passage of Scripture, think of it as happening in our inner being rather than being an outward, physical occurrence. Scripture will be in italics and my comments in regular font. Keep in mind that Jesus said, "…the kingdom of God is within you."

> *1 Th 4:13 But I would not have you to be ignorant, brethren, concerning them which are asleep, that ye sorrow not, even as others which have no hope.*

God does not want us to be ignorant concerning the fact that we have a spiritual body and a spiritual mind that are presently sleeping (them which are asleep). We are soon to enter (or are even now entering) a period of great tribulation such as the world has never known. This will be a time of such sorrows that many will totally despair of life itself and will choose to end their life. It will appear that there is absolutely no hope as there will be no place on earth where anyone can go to escape these sorrows. Even in the past few years we have seen natural disasters on a "scale of biblical proportions" according to the newscasters reporting on the tsunamis of Indonesia and Japan, the Chilean earthquake, the hurricanes, tornadoes, drought and flooding in the U.S., mudslides and other disasters worldwide. Terrorism and nuclear, biological and chemical weapons loom on the horizon along with threats of flu pandemics.

When we find ourselves in the midst of terrifying judgments, we will be greatly comforted when our spiritual body and mind begin to awaken. There is much for us to learn which cannot be explained here, but I know that the awakening of these heretofore unknown parts of our being will bring us great comfort. Their awakening will bring undeniable confirmation that Jesus is with us and we are beginning a process of transformation that will lead us into His kingdom. We will be entering into a realm of peace and safety never before known by humankind, yet we will still be on this earth. We will truly know that even now our citizenship is in heaven.

1 Th 4:14 For if we believe that Jesus died and rose again, even so them also which sleep in Jesus will God bring with him.

To understand this more fully, we need to look at the word "bring" in the Greek. In Greek the word for "bring" used here is *agō* which means "to lead." (By implication it means "bring," with "bring" being the English word chosen by the translators for this passage.) Now if we look at this verse replacing "bring" with "lead," it will make sense when we interpret them which sleep as being our spiritual body and unused portion of our mind which is spiritual. We could say that if we believe that Jesus died and rose again, in a similar way we can believe that the parts of us that are asleep and as good as dead in that we have no perception of them, Jesus will raise up and lead into His kingdom when He comes.

1 Th 4:15 For this we say unto you by the word of the Lord, that we which are alive and remain unto the coming of the Lord shall not prevent them which are asleep.

Here the word "prevent" (*phthano* in Greek) actually means "precede." We which are alive and remain refers to the parts of us we are now aware of—our natural body and mind. These parts of us will not rise first. Before they rise, we will become aware of our spiritual body awakening. At the same time, we will realize that our mind has a new capability to perceive things more spiritually than ever before. There will be a maturing of these parts that were formerly asleep until God determines it is time for the parts of us that are alive and remain (our natural body and mind) to be raised into a new dimension.

I'm sure this may be very difficult for many persons to understand, especially those who have frequently read or studied this passage and viewed it as being outward only. I know what I am seeing here is true because I have seen it many other places in the Scriptures; and I have been experiencing some of it. As described in chapter one of this book, my spiritual body has been awakened. I have been experiencing the opening of my spiritual mind in small but undeniable ways such as more spiritual dreams, visions and the opening of many scriptural passages that were previously closed to my understanding.

Additionally, the phenomenon of satanic ritual abuse and the resulting spiritual awakening we see as a result of it are proof that we have these parts of our bodies. The Devil cannot create anything. He can only take that which God created for His purposes and pervert and distort it. God made these parts of our being for a reason. What I am describing here in 1 Thessalonians is similar to 1 Corinthians 15 which states:

> *Behold, I show you a mystery; we shall not all sleep, but we shall all be changed, in a moment, in the twinkling of an eye, at the last trump: for the trumpet shall sound, and the dead shall be raised incorruptible, and we shall be changed. For this corruptible must put on incorruption, and this mortal must put on immortality. So when this corruptible shall have put on incorruption, and this mortal shall have put on immortality, then shall be brought to pass the saying that is written, Death is swallowed up in victory (1 Cor. 51-54).*

Once again, the dead here refers to our spiritual body and spiritual mind. These may be said to be dead or asleep...either way we are not aware of them and they are not active in this life in that we do not experience them until they are brought to life or awakened. As this passage reveals, these are capable of corruption. Those in satanic cults in whom these parts have been awakened, use them for evil purposes. This mortal, of course, refers to our physical body and earthly mind.

The Old Testament shows us in detail how we will be changed. I have found this in the four living creatures of Ezekiel (see my book *The Four Living Creatures*) and many other passages some of which are now video series posted on my website at www.hispresenceonline.org.

1 Th 4:16 For the Lord himself shall descend from heaven with a shout, with the voice of the archangel, and with the trump of God: and the dead in Christ shall rise first:

In Greek the word "shout" is *keleuma*, meaning "a cry of incitement, shout." Webster tells us "incitement" means "to set in motion, stir up, arouse." The Lord will stir up or arouse the spiritual body giving it a sensation of motion as I described previously. When this happens we will become aware of having a spiritual body for the first time.

With the voice of the archangel…Archangels make announcements from heaven. The word for "voice" is *phone* meaning "disclosure" as well as "noise, sound, or voice." This is a disclosure from heaven. Something is being made known to us that we have never before been able to comprehend because it is heavenly knowledge that can only be understood as our spiritual mind and body are awakened.

With the trump of God…trumpets are mentioned many places in Scripture and make an interesting study. The trumpet called the people to Mt. Sinai in Exodus where God manifested himself in thunder, lightening, clouds and the blast of the trumpet. (This was a frightening experience causing the people to tremble with fear. The second coming of Christ will not be fearful but will give us joy and peace beyond anything we have ever known.) In Isaiah the trumpet sounded a call to worship. In Revelation Christ's voice is "as of a trumpet." The trump of God here in 1 Thessalonians is calling us up closer to God into a different dimension and will bring us into a depth of worship and relationship beyond anything heretofore possible.

In the New Testament Greek the word "trump" or "trumpet" is defined as, "(through the idea of quavering or reverberation) a trumpet." Both "quaver" and "reverberate" are motion verbs. The motion I felt as my spiritual body was awakened could be likened to a slow quaver.

"Reverberate" means, according to the *Merriam-Webster Dictionary*, "to continue in or as if in a series of echoes; resound." The illustrative example they give is, "...an historic event that still *reverberates* today." That is certainly how I would describe what I have experienced. That exciting moment when I felt the gentle movement of my spiritual body still "reverberates" in me. I believe I experienced an historic event, and now I am writing about it so others will understand when it happens to them .

The message I received when my spiritual body was awakened could not have been more clearly conveyed to me if it had been a shout, a voice or a trumpet blast. Any of those would have frightened me. Imagine lying in your bed, quietly waiting for sleep when all of a sudden you hear a trumpet blast! Or someone shouts! What I experienced was "loud and clear" in the sense of conveying a message to me but at the same time gentle and comforting.

The dead in Christ shall rise first. As stated earlier, when viewing this inwardly the spiritual body and spiritual mind, of which we have not been aware, are being awakened unto a dimension of Spirit we have not known. We are not rising up spatially to a different geographical location somewhere in space; we are being awakened to a spiritual realm. It takes a physical body and mind to interact with our physical world. We require a spiritual body and spiritual mind to sense and comprehend a spiritual world.

There are those around us in satanic cults who have already been awakened to this realm. Because of the imperfection of their hearts, they are subject to the deception and torment of demons. Those who have been in cults but who are now in Christ (SRA persons) are able to occasionally comprehend the good spiritual dimensions also. Those Christians who pursue holiness and await God's call to awaken them to the heavenly dimensions will be in that realm perpetually, not just occasionally, yet they will not be subject to deception because their hearts will have been purified.

1 Th 4:17 Then we which are alive and remain shall be caught up together with them in the clouds, to meet the Lord in the air: and so shall we ever be with the Lord.

"Then we which are alive" refers of our physical body. We are alive because we have a physical body, but this body will be changed at the coming of the Lord, for this mortal must put on immortality (1 Cor 15:53).We see this also in Rom 8:11: "But if the Spirit of him that raised up Jesus from the dead dwell in you, he that raised up Christ from the dead shall also quicken your mortal bodies by his Spirit that dwelleth in you."There is no doubt that these physical bodies will have to be changed in order to enter into all God has for us at His second coming. When our bodies are changed, weapons of mass destruction and flu pandemics will no longer be a threat to us.

We who are alive and remain—"remain" is *perileipo* in Greek and means "survive." I believe "remain" here refers to the part of our soul that has survived the process of sanctification after the sin nature part of us has burned up in the purifying furnace of affliction. This is the part of our soul that has gained the right to pass into eternity because it has been sanctified and "meet for the master's use" (2 Tim 2:21).

*…Shall be caught up together with them in the clouds…*At this point we need to understand what clouds are. We know that literal clouds are merely collections of water vapor in the upper atmosphere. If we want to hold to a spatial, three dimensional view of the second coming, we can look up into the sky and expect to see Jesus standing or sitting on a cloud. Or we can take a more spiritual approach and ask ourselves the question, "What do clouds represent in Scripture?"

The word "cloud" or "clouds" appears 156 times in Scripture. Looking up every occurrence would make an interesting study. Also examining the word in the Hebrew and Greek languages may give us more insights. In Hebrew, the word for cloud used most often is 'anan, meaning "a cloud (as covering the sky), i.e. the nimbus or thunder-cloud." It is derived from a root word, 'anan, meaning "to cover; to cloud over; figuratively to act covertly, i.e. practice magic; enchanter, observer of times, soothsayer, sorcerer." (In the English derivation of the Hebrew word for "clouds" and its root word, the words look identical. However, in the actual Hebrew there is a part of one little diacritical mark that is missing on one of the words.)

Looking at this Hebrew definition of "clouds" does much to open our spiritual understanding of clouds. Clouds are something that cover over and block our view of things. Fog is nothing more than a cloud next to the earth that blocks our vision. Clouds block our view of the sun. I live in Western NY near Lake Ontario and the Finger Lakes. We have many days here when we never see the sun. Some people find this very depressing and move away or spend the winters somewhere else. I often think, "I'm glad the Son is shining in me or I'd have trouble living here too."

Once again, if we look for an inward explanation of a scripture that seems to be describing something outward, we will find a true spiritual understanding. Jesus, the Son, lives within us. A full manifestation of His presence to us is blocked by a covering, a cloud so to speak. This inner covering is called a veil. We have many layers of veils within us, the veil being our flesh.

This veil is mentioned in Hebrews 12: "Having therefore, brethren, boldness to enter into the holiest by the blood of Jesus, by a new and living way, which he hath consecrated for us, through the veil, that is to say, his flesh; And having an high priest over the house of God; let us draw near with a true heart in full assurance of faith, having our hearts sprinkled from an evil conscience, and our bodies washed with pure water." When Jesus died in the flesh, He made a way for those of us who still live in the flesh to enter into the presence of God. Notice that purity is required to enter in as we are to have "a true heart in full assurance of faith" and "having our hearts sprinkled from an evil conscience."

This veil is seen typically in the Old Testament in the tabernacle. There was a thick veil that separated the Holy Place from the Holy of Holies where the Ark of the Covenant (symbolizing the presence of

God) was located. Before the high priest could enter in once a year, he had to go through an elaborate cleansing ritual and wear specific clothing. On his forehead he wore a gold plate with the words "holiness unto the Lord" engraved on it. The high priest was a type of Jesus, and the veil in the temple was torn from top to bottom when Jesus died on the cross signifying that a way had been made for us to enter in also. We are now priests unto the Lord, but we must enter into His presence in purity and total holiness. We must be like Jesus in order to enter into His presence. We must pass through a thick veil made of many layers of our flesh in order to fully experience His presence in the spirit.

Now we understand that a cloud is a covering. The inward covering consists of the veils of our own flesh that block our vision of Jesus. Every circumstance and relationship in life affords us an opportunity to pass through a layer of the veil and come closer into God's presence. We must die to self in order for the veils to be removed. Jesus removes the veils, but only when we are willing to do our part by dying to our own self. If we are not progressing in holiness, the veils are not being removed.

If we look again at the Hebrew definition for clouds, we will notice that the root word from which it is derived not only means "to cover" but also incorporates an occult aspect related to sorcery, soothsaying and practicing magic. What could this have to do with clouds? Actually it has a lot to do with our spiritual understanding of clouds as being the veil of our flesh.

When people participate in occult activities such as fortune telling, séances, horoscopes or any of the myriad types of occult practices available (including Harry Potter books), veils are being removed by demons. (Jesus removes veils only when we are spiritually prepared for them to be removed. Demons remove them prematurely when we still have darkness in our hearts thereby opening our spirits up to demonic deception.) As the veils are gradually removed, they start believing they have "gifts" like extrasensory perception, clairvoyance, healing, etc. They are receiving their information and powers from demonic spirits, and their souls are headed for perdition. Some people who dabble a little in the occult, such as reading a few books but nothing more, may not seem to have gifts but they may become depressed or suffer other emotional problems because of the demons that now have permission to harass them. (Participation in anything occult is strictly forbidden [Deut. 18:10-12] and doing so opens us up to demonic torment.)

In my interpretation, *then we which are alive and remain shall be caught up together with them in the clouds* actually means this: Our spiritual body and spiritual mind are awakened first and raised up into the spiritual realm with Christ. Then our physical body and natural mind will follow, but first the veils of our flesh have to be removed. As we deny our self and follow Christ, Jesus removes these veils of flesh. Once again, if we think of this spatially, it will not make sense, but if we see that these parts of our self are not going away somewhere but are being raised spiritually, then it will be understandable.

We are to meet the Lord in the air. There are two Greek words translated "air." This particular word for "air" is *aer*, from *aemi* "(to breathe unconsciously, i.e. respire; by analogy to blow); 'air' (as naturally circumambient)." The air we breathe is very close to our body. The air spoken of here is not far off in the sky where birds fly as is another Greek word translated "air", *ouranos*, defined as "(elevation); the sky; heaven (as the abode of God); by implication happiness, power, eternity."

Aer, as found in the 1 Thessalonians passage, is the same word used by Paul when he said he did not fight as one beating the air. This would be the air close around him. Clearly this is not a catching up and disappearing off the face of the earth, but rather something that takes place right here. It is a catching up into a different realm that exists here but has been imperceptible to us. Once we have experienced this catching up we will be in a close face to face relationship with Jesus that supersedes anything we could have imagined. We will have experienced fully that He "is able to do exceedingly abundantly above all that we ask or think according to the power that worketh in us," and we will know experientially "the love of Christ, which passeth knowledge, that we might be filled with all the fullness of God." Then we will minister as Jesus would to a lost and dying world in the throes of end time tribulation.

If we view the second coming as an outward spatial event to be viewed with our natural eyes, then we tend to believe the particulars of the second coming will happen to everyone at the same time. However, we are not all spiritually ready for this experience at the same time. If we view it as occurring inwardly, then it becomes personal, intimate and relational as a bride and groom relationship should be. In this way persons can enter in at different times when they are spiritually mature and ready for a marriage relationship. And thankfully, the whole world won't be watching on CNN!

I realize I have written an interpretation of the second coming that has probably not been seen before; however, I deeply sense that the inward application is the correct mode of thinking for this difficult passage. I urge my readers to prayerfully consider what I have written and search the Scriptures to be as the Bereans who "received the word with all readiness of mind, and searched the scriptures daily, whether those things were so" (Acts 17:11).

The Desert—the Spiritual Body and the Occult

Persons deeply involved in occult activities know experientially about the existence of their spiritual body. During satanic rituals, demons separate the spirit from the soul and the spiritual body from the natural body. The spiritual body is awakened, along with all its senses, so that the spirit world is opened to be fully experienced.

Those of us who minister to satanically ritually abused persons see many things of a spiritual nature for which we have no explanation. Abused persons often don't understand the spiritual ramifications of their experience either—they just know they were abused and that they see and hear things other people don't. Most of them would be a lot happier if they didn't see and hear the things they do—demons appear to them, confusing voices speak to them, they feel evil spirit beings in, on and around their body—all of these things are not pleasant.

There is a flip side to all this misery, however. When they are with a Christian helper who calls upon the presence of Jesus to come and minister to them, they are able to perceive Him in a dimension those of us who were not abused don't experience. Many of them actually see Jesus, hear his voice and feel his touch. This is because their spiritual body, along with all their spiritual senses, has been awakened. It becomes obvious that there is a realm of spirit that people in satanic cults have entered that is foreign to most Christians. Certainly we don't want these terrible demonic experiences of the evil spiritual realm, but we desire to experience God's heavenly spiritual realm.

Participation in spiritual experiences forbidden by God, such as witchcraft, wizardry, séances, fortune telling, satanic rituals, etc., opens up this forbidden realm. All of us have within us a hunger for the supernatural. God intended for this hunger to lead us to Him. All too often people succumb to the temptation to seek out someone who purportedly has "gifts" of ESP, clairvoyance, etc. which are merely demons moving through certain individuals in order to deceive and entrap others. Participation in any of these activities causes us to pick up demons that begin to awaken the spiritual side of our being to forbidden areas of spirit that God intended only for his great Church of the end times. "I have many things to say unto you, but you cannot bear them now." The Church of the end times will hear many of these things as they come into the fullness of Christ.

Paul teaches in Ephesians Four, "And he gave some, apostles; and some, prophets; and some, evangelists; and some, pastors and teachers for the perfecting of the saints, for the work of the ministry, for the edifying of the body of Christ: till we all come in the unity of the faith, and of the knowledge of the Son of God, unto a perfect man, unto the measure of the stature of the fullness of Christ." Entering into the fullness of Christ will bring us into a realm of power and supernatural that far exceeds anything any Satanist ever dreamed of.

The fact that some have entered into something unrighteously reveals to the rest of us that there is something there to be entered. If it is there, it must have been created by God because Satan cannot create anything. He only perverts and distorts the good things created by God. If God created it, He intended it for good. There is a realm of supernatural waiting for the church of the end times. In order to enter this realm of spirit, we must die to the things of this world and walk in purity and holiness. Only then will God awaken the spiritual side of our being enabling us to perceive it. To enter before we are perfected in Him would only open us to demonic deception. Only God can lead us in.

God has many things to show us but most of us are too carnal at this point to receive them. Paul says in 1 Corinthians, "And I, brethren, could not speak unto you as unto spiritual, but as unto carnal, even as unto babes in Christ. I have fed you with milk, and not with meat: for hitherto ye were not able to bear it, neither yet now are ye able. For ye are yet carnal: for whereas there is among you envying, and strife, and divisions, are ye not carnal, and walk as men?"

When we Christians are willing to seek God with our whole heart by spending lengthy daily time in prayer and study (not merely reading) of the Word, walking in obedience and not loving the world, the supernatural of God becomes very evident. Being a Christian is the most exciting experience any person could ever hope for, but all too many Christians seem to have no testimony of the astounding, supernatural experiences that happen regularly when we walk closely with Christ.

When we minister to satanically ritually abused persons we begin to see, through their eyes, things that others don't see. We become aware of the depths of evil going on in our society right under our noses. We see the unwillingness of many persons to believe this is actually happening. In other words, we begin to see beneath the surface of society. We have information others don't have and don't want to have.

As our eyes are opened to these things (and this is a righteous opening of our eyes because we are not directly seeking cult experiences but only helping those abused by them) we see how totally wicked demons are as they manifest in our survivors. We actually see that the word of God is the sword of the Spirit. We quote Scriptures and the demons flee from our survivors in terror. We speak the name of Jesus, and watch them writhe and sneer in disgust and terror at the power of that Name. (I want to make clear that we only see the manifestations if a demon takes over the body of the person to whom we are ministering.)

Not only do we see demons through our survivors, but we also see Jesus in a way others do not see Him. My SRA friends tell me about His love as little child alters are taken by Jesus, gently washed in the sparkling waterfalls of heaven and clothed in beautiful white dresses. Perhaps He gives them a little kitten to hold or a gentle, belled lamb to pet. One who fears the dark may be given a flashlight or perhaps granted to see a large guardian angel watching over her. The glimpses of Jesus we see through SRA persons are very precious indeed. We are allowed to see into realms of spirit that would otherwise be closed to us, but when we are perfected, God will awaken our spiritual body and senses to see these things also.

These deeper levels of seeing are blessings God gives to those who are willing to make the sacrifices necessary to minister to SRA persons. At the same time, we should be careful to stay in the Word so we will be balanced and well grounded in truth to help insure we don't become deceived by the mystifying spiritual things we hear and see through our survivors.

CHAPTER EIGHT

Astral Projection and Soul/Spirit Travel

One sees many strange things when ministering to satanically ritually abused persons. One of the strangest is when voices speak out of them claiming to be the spirit or soul of some other human being. These beings will have personalities and mannerisms characteristic of the person they claim to be. It all looks and sounds very convincing to the minister pondering whether or not this could possibly be true.

Additionally one hears accounts of human spirit or soul travel known as astral projection or out-of-the-body experiences. Persons speak of seeing a thin silver cord connecting them to their body while they are having their out-of-the-body experience. They are not speaking of a near-death experience, but rather soul travel in that a person goes somewhere and sees and experiences things apart from his physical body.

When Christians search the Bible for an explanation of this strange phenomenon, they quite likely will come upon a verse in Ecclesiastes that may seem to confirm that astral projection really happens. Speaking of death, this passage states, "Or ever the silver cord be loosed, or the golden bowl be broken, or the pitcher be broken at the fountain, or the wheel broken at the cistern. Then shall the dust return to the earth as it was: and the spirit shall return unto God who gave it." However, it is important to note that this passage is speaking about death. There is nothing about astral projection implied here.

Is it possible for a human soul or spirit to travel out of the body and project itself into another person? Many persons who minister for satanic ritual abuse believe this to be true. One counselor related to me that he led the soul of an abuser to salvation as he talked to it when it manifested in the body of the SRA person to whom he was ministering. There are some who say they were raped by human spirits or thrown around the room by them.

There are many reasons why I do not believe a person's soul or spirit leaves his body and travels around or enters into the physical body of another person. For one thing, the Bible makes no mention of such a thing. It does say that a demon can leave a human body, travel and come back in.

> *When the unclean spirit is gone out of a man, he walketh through dry places, seeking rest; and finding none, he saith, I will return unto my house whence I came out. And when he cometh, he findeth it swept and garnished. Then goeth he, and taketh to him seven other spirits more wicked than himself; and they enter in, and dwell there: and the last state of that man is worse than the first (Luke 11:24- 26).*

If human souls or spirits were entering in and out of other people or accosting them, surely the Bible would have something to say about such an important concept. Paul in 2 Corinthians where he speaks of being caught up into paradise says, "Whether in the body, or out of the body, I cannot tell: God knoweth." Whether or not Paul was in or out of his body, it was an experience with God, not with other humans on earth and therefore cannot be an example of astral projection.

People truly believe they are having this experience of soul travel, but it is a delusion. Spiritual dreams and visions often seem incredibly real. It is not uncommon for a survivor to whom I am ministering to report having dreams in which I abuse them. These dreams are so real they have trouble believing they never happened. This is merely a tactic of the enemy to try to get them to break off our relationship. I've never been abused, but I've had spiritual dreams such that, upon awakening, I didn't know for a few minutes whether or not they really happened. These dreams for me have been from the Lord and have had a deep impression on me.

Visions can come in different forms. Some can be revelations that come with a conscious sense of the presence of the Lord. Some people have had visions that seemed to be as though they were watching a movie. Then there is the kind of vision where the person feels like they are actually in the movie. A trance seems real like a dream but happens when the person is awake. Peter had a trance at the time he was instructed to go to the house of Cornelius. Paul experienced a trance as described in Acts 22. All of these occurred without the person leaving their body.

If God can give people trances, the Devil can give trances to those whom he has been able to deceive. A person can go into a trance and believe he is experiencing leaving his body and traveling to some distant place where he interacts with other persons. Demons know about the scripture that speaks of a silver cord, so they show a silver cord connected to the body as the soul or spirit of the person "leaves." Demons are able to give a number of people a similar trance at the same time and make them believe they met somewhere when they "astral projected."

Why, one might ask, would the Devil do such a thing? Why deceive people and make them believe their soul or spirit left their body and traveled? This deception is of great benefit to the enemy in regards to satanic ritual abuse. If Satan is able to make a counselor believe the spirit he is encountering in an SRA person is human, then the counselor believes he cannot control the spirit (or soul) and cast it out. We have authority over demons but we do not have authority over the soul or spirit of a human being. In this way the demons trick the counselor into believing he cannot cast them out or tell them what to do. I have cast out every evil spirit that told me he was a person. If

I believed it was really a human spirit, I would not have faith to cast it out.

I have had SRA counselors tell me that human spirits come and rape and assault some of their survivors. This should not be! It has never happened to the people I minister to. The reason it happens to their survivors is that they and the counselor believe human souls have astral projected and are doing these things. Actually this is all demonic activity.

The counselor who related to me that he led the soul of an abuser to Christ as he manifested through an SRA person was not willing to even listen to my explanation of what may have happened. He was totally closed to any suggestion that it could have been anything else. He said there was no way that any demon would renounce Satan, pray the sinner's prayer, confess sins and ask for forgiveness. He said he had seen it all with his own eyes and he knew it was true.

I too have seen these manifestations of human spirits in SRA persons. They are extremely convincing, but I realize the power and craftiness of evil spirits. They have no loyalty to Satan or anyone else. Satan would probably congratulate a demon for deceiving the counselor by renouncing him, faking repentance and prayer. The whole experience described above gave incredible power to the belief that human spirits can accost people and thereby opened the door for powerful demons to harass and assault this man's counselees. He could also convince other counselors about his belief in his experience and without intending to, open a door for their survivors to be accosted also.

This counselor who related the experience of leading a human soul to Christ through a survivor assured me that many counselors believe this and there are tapes and articles explaining why it is all true. After receiving a few of this man's emails, I pondered it all for an entire day and continually asked God to show me if I was wrong. I thought I had had the matter all settled but I needed to be absolutely sure.

That night I had a dream. In my dream there was a man over the Internet who was trying to sell me a string of beads. I had a friend who had bought them, but I was more cautious, and as I looked closely at the beads, I could see there was something defective about them… their surface was slightly marred. I decided not to buy them.

When I awoke and considered the message of the dream, it all became clear to me. The beads represented the concept of astral projection and human souls projected into other humans that the counselor related to me. With deception, one false belief leads to another and another like a string of beads. My friend who had bought them I knew to be a fine Christian woman but a little naïve. God was showing me this whole concept was defective and I was not to "buy it."

Adam's Soul Power

Some persons believe in something called "the latent power of the human soul." This concept suggests that Adam had incredible soul powers as evidenced by his ability to name all the animals and dress and keep the garden. This soul power was lost when Adam and Eve through their own sin cast all creation into sin, and death came upon all living things. It is taught that humans still have this power within but it is locked up in our flesh. There are certain individuals who have been able to suppress their body to such an extent that they have been able to utilize this latent power of their soul.

I also believe Adam had powers we do not have. However, my explanation for this is that his spiritual side which died (or went to sleep) at the time of the fall, was in union with God. This unity (and the power that went with it as emanating from God) was lost to him when his spiritual side died.

Some latent powers of the soul are believed to include clairvoyance—the power to perceive things which are out of the natural range of human senses; telepathy—communication by scientifically unknown or inexplicable means such as thought reading; psychometry—the ability to read the past like an open book; and statuvolism—the ability to "throw one's mind" to any distant place and see, hear, feel, smell and taste what is going on there.

I have encountered these phenomena in SRA persons and found these powers to be demons. Once the demon was cast out, the person lost the ability to do these things. If one believes these are soul powers, one might be tempted to try developing these powers and could find themselves enslaved to demons.

As I was writing this, my daughter who lives in another state called to tell me something that just happened in her home. Her teenage daughter was watching television and called to her mother about something she was viewing. A man on the program told a woman to open a dictionary, mentally choose a word, and then close the book. The man was able to tell the woman the exact word she had chosen.

My granddaughter asked, "Mom, how did he do that?" My daughter replied, "Demons are all around in the place. A demon saw the word the woman chose and told the man." "Oh," said my granddaughter. "I thought it was something like that." That settled the matter and the issue had been dealt with.

What if my daughter had said, "That man practiced until he was able to subdue his flesh to the point that the latent power of his soul was released. That was possible because he has been able to gain back some of the power of the soul that Adam had before the fall. This potential is in all of us if we could only learn to use it."

My granddaughter would have had a lot to ponder. She may have thought, "Gee, if I could do that people would admire me as someone really special. I'd be the life of the party." If she had tried to pursue this power, she would have put herself in contact with demons.

An examination of the New Testament Greek words translated "power" indicates that power comes from sources outside of human ability. The two most common words for power are *dunamis* and *exousia*. The following are taken from *The New Strong's Expanded Exhaustive Concordance of the Bible:*

Dunamis – force, miraculous power. *Dunamis* almost always points to new and higher forces that have entered and are working in this lower world of ours.

Exousia – authority...superhuman, delegated influence.

There are two other New Testament Greek words for "power" that are used less often:

Kratos – force, might, strength. *Kratos* means might, relative and manifested power chiefly from God.

Chalchalah – the strength of God bestowed upon believers. The visible expression of the inherent personal power of the Lord Jesus. It is said of angels. It is ascribed to God.

Clearly these Greek words with their definitions show that power comes from outside our human soul.

The idea that the human soul can leave the body and travel around is further refuted by the biblical explanation for the Old Testament Word translated "soul." The Hebrew word for soul, נפש, *nephesh*, indicates that the soul and the body are bound up closely together in such a way that the soul could not leave the body except in death. The following is from the introduction to *Gesenius' Hebrew-Chaldee Lexicon to the Old Testament*:

According to the Genesis account of creation, after "the Lord God formed man of the dust of the ground and breathed into his nostrils the breath of life," man became "a living soul" (2:7). What does the word soul mean? Or more precisely, what does the Hebrew word mean that is translated "soul"?

The first and most basic definition of נפש is breath. The second definition is more complex: the soul, or that vital principle "by which the body lives, the token of which life is drawing breath...hence life..." From this definition it is apparent that the concept of the soul is bound up closely with that of the body. The third definition is the mind, the whole inner being with all its faculties. Yet the mind and all its inner motions cannot be known by men apart from its employment of the body and the five senses, which fact is implied in this definition. The fourth definition is animal, "that in which there is a soul or mind…living creature…There is something that all the various species of the animal world have in common with man: they are breathing bodies or living creatures. Thus שׁפנ points to the body as well as the inner being, the vital principle, and the breath of a creature or person. The fifth definition is summarized by the word self and the various ways in which self is used, singular or plural, with or without pronominal prefixes. Self basically means "the whole person or entire being of an individual." According to the Bible the human soul is the whole human personality, composed of a breathing body and all of man's inner faculties, expressly created by God to bear His own image and likeness. (Gesenius 1979, vi)

From this explanation of the Hebrew word for "soul," it is clear that the soul is the life, the breath and the vital principle by which the body lives. The soul cannot leave the body and travel around or project itself into another person.

In Ecclesiastes Ten there is an interesting verse that states, "Curse not the king, no not in thy thought; and curse not the rich in thy bedchamber: for a bird of the air shall carry the voice, and that which hath wings shall tell the matter."

Birds in Scripture are sometimes used allegorically of demons. The parable of the soils in Matthew Thirteen is a good example: "And he spake many things unto them in parables, saying, Behold, a sower went forth to sow; and when he sowed, some seeds fell by the way side, and the fowls came and devoured them up." Jesus then explained the meaning as, "When any one heareth the word of the kingdom, and understandeth it not, then cometh the wicked one, and catcheth away that which was sown in his heart." Birds are likened to the evil one… the Devil or his demons.

This passage reveals that the one who is spying on people in the Ecclesiastes verse is not a human soul projected into the room, but probably a demon. If a human soul could be there in the bedchamber reading one's mind and listening to their voice, wouldn't Scripture indicate this somewhere? Scripture does verify it could be a demon.

In 2 Kings there is a remarkable account of Elisha knowing the enemy's battle plans and relaying them to the king of Israel. With this information the king of Israel was able to save himself from the king of Syria many times. In exasperation the Syrian king called his men together demanding to know who the traitor was in their midst. One of them answered, "None, my lord, O king: but Elisha, the prophet that is in Israel, telleth the king of Israel the words that thou speakest in thy bedchamber."

The Syrians went to destroy Elisha and surrounded the city where he was during the night. When daylight came and Elisha's servant saw them, he was terrified. Elisha's response was, "Fear not for they that be with us are more than they that be with them." Scripture continues, "And the LORD opened the eyes of the young man; and he saw: and behold, the mountain was full of horses and chariots of fire round about Elisha. And when they came down to him, Elisha prayed unto the LORD and said, Smite this people, I pray thee, with blindness according to the word of Elisha." The Lord blinded them and the rest of the story can be read in 2 Kings 6.

The point I want to make here is that Elisha's miracles were all done by prayer with heavenly angelic beings and the Holy Spirit performing them. Some might believe Elisha projected his soul into the king of Syria's bedchamber, but this is in no way implied in this account. Elisha knew what was being said because he was a man of prayer to whom God revealed secrets.

As to the soul having power to do miraculous things, principles learned during SRA ministry reveal that power is not from the soul but from the demons controlling the soul. This is why the survivor who has the greatest dissociative ability will be the person with the greatest powers. Each alter formed will have possibly four to eight (or more) demons attached to her. The greater the number of alters, the more demons can be attached...and demons are powers. Paul said in Ephesians Six, "For we wrestle not against flesh and blood, but against principalities, against *powers*, against the rulers of the darkness of this world, against spiritual wickedness in high places" (italics mine).

If one personality had 6000 demons (approximately the number in the Gadarene demoniac of Mark 5), there is no way all those demons could each have a turn at controlling the person. (For my explanation of why I believe this man was SRA, please see my first book, *Restoring Survivors of Satanic Ritual Abuse.*) They would be continually fighting over who got to be in control. But when there are many personalities, and each personality has a small number of demons, each demon gets to control someone. There is always the strongman in charge of the lesser demons. In this way, the inner world is kept in order and there is greater power.

To sum it all up, I have noticed that survivors whose counselors believe in astral projection and human souls projecting into other persons, have trouble with harassment from these "human souls." People may be raped or thrown around the room in terrible abuse. However, I don't believe in this, and it doesn't happen to the people I minister to, or if it happens, it is only once. When I hear about it, I cast the demon out. This is because I know these are demons and can, therefore, take authority over them. If I believed they were human souls or spirits and that I had no authority over them, I could not help my survivors. It is my prayer that my writing on this subject will help destroy this widespread and dangerous belief in soul projection.

People who minister to those who have been satanically ritually abused are seeing behind the veil through their survivors. Demon powers are confronted continually. These spiritual beings will deceive us if we are not careful to continually search the Scriptures to find the truth behind the strange phenomena we are encountering in this ministry. If we believe something on the basis of what we and others are observing apart from biblical explanations, we will be led into deception.

The Sea

Let's take another look at our Ezekiel verse:

Then said he unto me, These waters issue out toward the east country, and go down into the desert, and go into the sea: which being brought forth into the sea, the waters shall be healed (Ezekiel 47:8).

The living waters of the presence of Jesus have been healing the physical body (country), opening unused portions of the mind (loins), and awakening the spiritual body (desert); now these waters go into the sea causing the sea to be healed. The sea is representative of our restless desires, "…the wicked are like the troubled sea, when it cannot rest, whose waters cast up mire and dirt. There is no peace, saith my God, to the wicked" (Isa. 57:20, 21).

While we are still indwelt with a carnal nature, we have desires springing up from deep within our heart that are opposed to the will of God—desires such as wanting to be acknowledged by others, wanting to be successful according to man's standards, desiring more material goods, etc. These restless desires cause many needless storms in our lives since our will in these areas is opposed to the will of God. As the healing waters of the Spirit flow into these areas of our being, our desires are changed from selfish, carnal ones to a pure desire for the will of God alone. When our desires line up with God's, the storms cease and the waters are healed.

Satanists are driven by their restless desires for power, wealth and recognition. It is difficult for those of us who are used to the gentle promptings of the Holy Spirit to comprehend the relentless driving force of the demonically empowered evil desires of the wicked. Truly there is no peace (Isa. 48:22) or sweet sleep (Prov. 3:24) for those so driven. Imagine working at a job all day, then being up at a satanic ritual from midnight till 4:00 a.m. and then going back to the job at 7:00 a.m. after about two hours sleep. Sometimes, during important satanic holidays, rituals go on every night for perhaps a week.

As we think of these desires being like the troubled sea, we can picture the unceasing, relentless force of the waves as they crash against the shore, robbing it of its sand, pulling houses off their foundations and sweeping them out to sea. The Hebrew word for "troubled" is *garish*, meaning "to drive out from a possession." The life God has given them is no longer their possession but has become the Devil's. Only God can calm a troubled sea. Satanists experience a degree of relief from their driving desires immediately after a ritual but it is not long before they are compelled to have another.

A Multitude of Fish

Continuing on with verse nine we read,

> *And it shall come to pass, that every thing that liveth, which moveth, whithersoever the rivers shall come, shall live: and there shall be a very great multitude of fish, because these waters shall come thither: for they shall be healed; and every thing shall live whither the river cometh (Ezekiel 47:9).*

As Andrew Jukes reveals in his book, *Types in Genesis*, fish are the emotions that spring forth from our desires. Now that the desires of our heart have been aligned with the desires of God's heart, our emotions are healed. Prior to the healing of our desires, emotions have been one of our greatest problems for what person has been able to truly control their emotions? We have denied them, buried them, built walls to hide from them, only to see them erupt again in different forms in our addictions and stress related illnesses. Only God can righteously control and heal our emotions. In this passage of Ezekiel, the emotions (fish) are finally healed as the healing river flows into the sea (desires).

This Hebrew word for "healed," *rapha*, means "to mend by stitching." The first thing Adam and Eve did after they sinned and realized they were naked, was sew. They were stitching fig leaves together trying to hide their nakedness when God called out to them asking where they were.

The first and immediate result of their sin was emotion—negative emotions of shame, degradation, unworthiness, fear, etc. These emotions were spawned from their evil desire to be independent of God. Their immediate response to these emotions was to hide from the presence of God. These same emotions have been keeping us from the presence of God ever since, and like Adam and Eve, we too have been stitching fig leaves together, attempting to heal our emotions by our own efforts. However, in these last days, God will be doing the stitching as He binds us to Himself like many threads of a tapestry sewn together. His life will be so interwoven (stitched) with our life, we will become as one. His desires will have become our desires, then His pure emotions will be flowing abundantly through us.

With the healing of our emotions will come the realization we have buried or shut off many feelings in an effort to protect ourselves from pain. When emotional pain has come, we have all consciously or unconsciously attempted to turn off or numb our feelings. In so doing, we have not only lessened the pain but squelched the good feelings as well. As the emotions are healed, all our defense mechanisms will go. Now it will be safe to turn loose of these defenses because, with the loving presence of Jesus so manifest to our senses, we need fear these emotions no longer. Many emotions that have seemed dead will begin to live. We will be free to experience a great multitude of emotions because fear of pain and our numbing defense mechanisms will be gone. At this juncture, love, joy, peace, tenderness, compassion, etc. will be greatly multiplied in our life. We will enjoy a depth of emotion never before known to any man as "joy unspeakable and full of glory" floods our entire being.

A Multitude of Fish—Evil Emotions

After hearing hundreds of memories about dysfunctional satanic homes, I would have to say the predominant ruling emotion in a Satanist is anger. Anger was the prevailing emotion in Cain when God accepted Abel's offering but rejected Cain's. Cain was not a Satanist so far as we know, but his offering was not pleasing to God. People who know they are living a life that God cannot respect are often angry people.

When God did not respect Cain's offering, "Cain was wroth and his countenance fell" (Gen. 4:7). The Hebrew word for "wroth," is *charah* meaning "to blaze up with anger or jealousy," "to fret self," "grieve." These are not pleasant emotions and they describe those who have chosen to worship Satan.

When the desires are wicked, the emotions that spring from those desires are all unpleasant. People do experience a kind of euphoria during the rituals or when they are committing acts of wickedness, but it soon fades away and the torment of hell returns.

The emotions in the healing river are healed and all of them live, but in the opposite river from the serpent's mouth, the emotions are unhealthy and many are dead. All the good emotions such as joy, contentment, compassion, or meekness are dead—absolutely nonexistent. When one hears the memories of the SRA, one cannot help but notice the total absence of any good or seemingly human emotions in the perpetrators. As the demons take over the people, they become like vicious, starved wild animals with a total absence of decency, compassion or mercy. As I have listened to these memories, I have been amazed at the total absence of anything considered human in the perpetrators, not only in the ritual but also at home. When the demons surface during ministry, I see the same thing in them— unbelievable coldness and cruelty.

Satanists, being human, do have to manage their own emotions, all of which are unpleasant, and so are driven to seek ways of dealing with their pain. They may resort to alcohol, drugs, food, etc., much like the average person, but they also have twisted, evil ways of relieving their pain by performing acts of extreme violence in rituals, at home to family members, or to strangers in society. They cannot find peace or rest unless they do Satan's evil bidding to harm another human being or animal in some way. In the home, these acts of violence frequently erupt in rape, torture, beatings and mental cruelty.

The torment for a child born into some satanic families is not limited to the rituals; it goes on at home all day long and into the night. There is no safe place to hide and no time of day that is free from abuse. Children may be brutally dragged out of bed, beaten and raped in the middle of the night or taken from their bed to a vicious ritual where they are tortured and raped. One dear woman to whom I ministered, had a few alters who were kittens. In her extreme suffering as a child on the farm, she tried to convince herself she was a kitten because they were ignored. This is the kind of desperation experienced by a child for whom there is absolutely no place of safety and no person to turn to for help.

Not all satanic families are this cruel at all times. In some families there are no acts of outward physical violence in the course of a typical day. All the violence may take place only in rituals. There is suffering of a different type that is ongoing though…things like indifference, lack of encouragement or compassion, legalism, control, etc.

Fishers Stand from Engedi to Eneglaim

And it shall come to pass, that the fishers shall stand upon it from Engedi even unto Eneglaim; they shall be a place to spread forth nets; their fish shall be according to their kinds, as the fish of the great sea, exceeding many (Ezekiel 47:10).

This word "fishers" is found only one other place in Scripture, in Jeremiah 16:16, where fishers are seen as an instrument of judgment used by God against His rebellious people. This verse in Ezekiel (and the next) will reveal God's judgment on the remaining carnality in the life of the believer. The Hebrew word for "stand," *'amad,* also means "appointed," so our spiritual interpretation could read, "And it shall come to pass that judgment shall be appointed from Engedi to Eneglaim."

The name "Engedi" means "the place of the young goat" *(Holman Bible Dictionary, QuickVerse)*. Since the goat's head often represents satanic entities and Christ divides the sheep from the goats, goats would be a bad thing to have within. This specifically means "young" goats so I'm thinking this represents the source of our sin nature. It is something within us that breeds and produces goats if you will. When Christ judges this, we will no longer have the tendency towards sin within our nature that came upon us all at the fall of Adam.

At one time Engedi was called Hazazontamar which means "division of the palm trees." Men are allegorically referred to as "trees" in scripture, e.g. the blind man who saw men as trees, walking (Mark 8). We are the palm trees and we are going to be divided from our flesh in the final judgment, and as this takes place, we will come to Eneglaim.

Eneglaim, a place mentioned nowhere else in Scripture but here, means "a fountain of two calves." In Scripture a calf is a sacrificial animal. Our lives are to be lived as a sacrifice in two ways...a sacrifice unto God and a sacrifice unto others. As we choose to lay down our life in this way, a fountain of living waters will flow out of us straight from God. This living water will not only flow out to others but also to us. We will experience God's presence and love in a way reserved for His bride, the Church of the end times.

Fishers—Judgment

Every human being will be judged by God. People tend to think this will happen only after death, but it should be transpiring now in the life of every believer. The Bible tells us that if we would judge ourselves, we would not be judged (1 Cor. 11:31). The more sensitive our spirit is to God, the more quickly we can discern sin in our life and turn from it; therefore, God can be more gentle in His judging because a sensitive conscience will immediately know when it has offended God and repent. At some point in these end times, the Lord will actually remove the sin nature as we just saw in the words Engedi, Hazazontamar, and Eneglaim.

The wicked will suffer tremendously at their time of judgment when they are sentenced to hell for a life of wickedness and rebellion toward God. They are incapable of judging themselves because they are deceived and believe in their heart "I shall not be moved: for I shall never be in adversity" (Psalm 10:6).

When I listen to memories of what evil people have done to innocent children, I sometimes wonder if there is a place in hell hot enough for them. Then I, along with my survivor friend, have to repent and forgive them and remember that our enemy is the Devil not the people.

Most of the perpetrators involved in the deepest wickedness of SRA were probably horribly abused as children themselves. Much of Satanism today is generational with whole families having been raised in it for generations. All the children in these families are subjected to the terror of rituals replete with all the torture, death and sexual sin imaginable. They must decide to become either a victim or a perpetrator. Those who choose the side of evil and participate in the wickedness willingly are relieved of most of the abuse in the home and at the rituals. Others cannot bring themselves to harm others and then suffer greatly as a result. Truly those who participate in Devil-worship and harm others are to be held accountable for their actions, but at the same time we should have compassion for them knowing their childhood was anything but normal.

I believe even the perpetrators have dissociated into different personality parts. During the day in public, they can appear kind, considerate and hardworking, but at home, or in the rituals, another evil self comes forth that is capable of the greatest wickedness. Unless we as believers walk in the deepest discernment of God's Spirit, we will not recognize who these people are. Nevertheless, we are not to fear because if we are obedient to God, He will guide our steps and protect us from harm even though we don't know who they are. We must pray, ask God to direct us through each day and trust Him to guide our steps.

It takes faith and maturity to know how to handle the information about satanic people that one hears in the memories of the SRA. Sometimes the names of prominent people in the community come up in memories and you find yourself privy to information others don't have. Then you want to warn others in order to protect them because some of those names will be those of doctors, officials or persons in authority in your community.

Over the years God has taught me to leave all these matters in His hands and live my life as though I know nothing. For example, there is a funeral home beside a cemetery I used to drive past almost every day. I have heard memories from several people about satanic rituals that occur there. I have said nothing about it but these memories have been confirmed through my observations of a close SRA friend who is frequently in the car with me. Whenever we go past that particular place, she feels demons jump on her unless I'm praying for her as we go past. My husband and others in our church have noticed that cars coming onto the highway from the road beside this cemetery are reckless. Many times they completely ignore the stop sign or if they stop, they then pull out in front of us making us jam on our brakes.

The people in our church know about this place but when it comes to others in our community, we have to trust that God will protect them. If we were to sound an alarm, most people would not believe us, and we would be subjected to ridicule, gossip and perhaps endangerment to our lives without having benefited anyone. God wants us to focus on Him, listen to the memories, and then live a normal life.

There is a time to speak out, however, and that is when information comes forth indicating children are being abused. In such cases one must speak out after praying and receiving guidance from the Holy Spirit.

CHAPTER NINE

The Spreading of Nets

Continuing on with verse 10:

> *...they shall be a place to spread forth nets; their fish shall be according to their kinds, as the fish of the great sea, exceeding many (Ezekiel 47:10).*

The word "place" is not in the Hebrew so won't enter into our spiritual understanding. The word for "nets," *cherem,* is also translated "devoted." It is the same word found in Lev. 27:21, "But the field, when it goeth out in the jubilee, shall be holy unto the LORD, as a field *devoted...*" And again in Lev. 27:28, "...every *devoted* thing is most holy unto the Lord" (italics mine).

The understanding here is that spreading over all the emotions (fish) is a devotion to the Lord (net); there is holiness of emotions. All emotions are being caught up to the Lord as fish are caught up in a net. Every emotion is perfectly aligned with the heart of God and centered in His eternal Being.

No longer will our emotions be swayed by any carnal persuasion. The enemy cannot tempt us emotionally in an attempt to lead us astray because there will be a perfecting of all emotions and with this perfecting will come multiplication and great abundance of emotions. Emotions that have been limited before, e.g. the ability to love others, will be greatly enhanced and know no bounds. Compassion will flow forth out of us as it did from Jesus. Joy and peace will be unlimited.

We need to understand that the magnitude of blessing the Lord has for His people in these last days is immeasurably vast, so that when we experience the trials of death to self necessary to come into all this, we can be like Jesus who "for the joy that was set before him endured the cross…" (Hebrews 12:2).

The Spreading of Nets—No Control

The emotions of the wicked, rather than being under control as in a net, rage out of control, subject to the whims of demons. Satanists are deceived into believing their emotions are under their control because they can commit the greatest atrocities against humanity without flinching; but the truth is, all the good emotions are dead and the wicked emotions are driven by demons forcing the humans to commit acts of gross wickedness. The following passages from the New Living Translation vividly describe the emotional plight of those ensnared in Satanism.

- Evil people cannot sleep until they have done their evil deed for the day. They cannot rest unless they have caused someone to stumble. They eat wickedness and drink violence (Prov. 4:16,17).
- An evil man is held captive by his own sins; they are ropes that catch and hold him. He will die for lack of self-control; he will be lost because of his incredible folly (Prov. 5:22,23).
- The fears of the wicked will all come true (Prov. 10:24).
- The expectations of the wicked are all in vain (Prov. 10:28b).
- Wickedness never brings stability; only the godly have deep roots (Prov. 12:3).
- The words of the wicked are like a murderous ambush (Prov. 12:6).

Evil Satan worshipers are attempting to cooperate with one another and coordinate their efforts to destroy all the good in the world and usher in the reign of the Antichrist; but how can treacherous lying people work together to accomplish anything when they are all out for themselves at the expense of others? Several answers come to mind:

- They are held together by a great deceptive goal—the lie that they will rule the world alongside the Antichrist.
- God has allowed Satanism to continue because God's ultimate purpose for the Church will be achieved through it. His people will rise up in strength and power, as they stand undaunted against the greatest evil of all time.
- The punishment for betrayal in the cults is so horrendous very few dare fail in their assignments or attempt to leave. Most of them have seen the slow dismemberment and agonizing death experienced by traitors.
- Because Satanists cannot trust one another, they don't want to store valuable data on computer discs or microchips that could easily be lost, stolen, sold or used for blackmail. Their way around this problem is to store the data in human beings!

Those who minister to survivors of satanic ritual abuse know that when memories of atrocious abuse surface, the person often remembers every minute detail of the entire episode. It could be likened to a time capsule with the whole experience perfectly preserved—locked in time—and then experienced again many years later during ministry. It is amazing to hear and see someone during such a memory because they know precisely what everyone was wearing, where they were positioned, the details of the surroundings, the exact words spoken along with the emotional and physical pain. Every detail of the entire episode is remembered perfectly as though it had just happened.

Knowledge of this phenomenon is used by the Satanists for the purpose of storing data in their SRA victim. The person is traumatized to the point she splits and forms an alternate personality. That alter is named, given an identification code known only by the cult and then forced to memorize enormous amounts of data—it could be maps, lists of names, detailed instructions for various covert enterprises, etc. Once they are sure the information is perfectly memorized, they viciously traumatize their subject again to cause her to split away from that alter. All the information is locked up in that particular alter accessible only by those who know her specific identification code. In this way, vast amounts of data are "safely" stored away in a "spiritual" dimension. Should accusations ever be made, there would be no evidence that could be brought forth in a court of law.

Cultists know that should this person try to tell anyone about her abuse, they would think she was mentally ill, medicate her and perhaps lock her away in a mental hospital. In fact, certain alters are programmed to act as though suffering from extreme mental illness to ensure this will indeed take place. There is no way anyone would believe that this "emotionally ill" person had "data banks" of voluminous material stored away in her unconscious mind or that it could be accessed by people who know the codes that trigger the alters. An example comes to mind.

My husband and I once spent an evening with a fellow pastor and his wife when the subject of satanic ritual abuse came up. They mentioned that several years ago a woman had called their church from another state claiming to have been satanically ritually abused and asking for help. The associate pastor who took the call was alarmed and called several intercessors to pray for her. Subsequent calls were made in an attempt to help this woman. She said her father was a prominent doctor in their city and also her main abuser. In the course of trying to help this woman, the senior pastor called the father and talked to him. The father said his daughter was mentally ill and had been hospitalized several times because of it. The doctor was, of course, very educated and polite and the pastor believed him. This woman never received help…at least not from this particular church.

This is the plight of those so abused. Their upbringing is filled with trauma. Love and touch are denied, and the result is as expected—a person with deep emotional and psychological problems who may be in and out of mental hospitals all her life. No one is going to believe her if she tries to speak of her abuse because it is so outrageously horrendous, no one will believe it. Now add to that the fact that she may have vast stores of valuable information locked away in her unconscious mind that can be accessed via certain codes and now, not only will she be considered "mentally ill," but so might anyone who believes this!

Now add to this information the fact that there are "Christian" men traveling all over the world who feel "called" to help the satanically ritually abused. Their method of counseling is to use codes to trigger alters and programming in their clients. They also find out about other satanic codes through the alters they trigger in these people. They add this information to their big notebook and travel on to the next person. Are they really helping anyone or are they just getting information? I'll let the reader decide.

I want to add here that most likely God will not let any godly counselor have the cult data stored away in the alters. It is His way of protecting us from information we should not have. The first woman I ministered to for SRA had a phenomenal ability to split and form alters, so she was greatly used by the cult to store information. We both thought God would give us that information once we reached the lowest level of her inner world where she had eighteen computers filled with data. (Satanists highly skilled in mind control can make an alter believe she is a computer or anything else that suits the cult's purposes.) The Lord delivered those alters and then wiped out their information. We never learned anything. I was disappointed at the time, but now I realize it is best that I know nothing. If I had the information, what would I do with it? No one would believe me anyway and my life might be greatly endangered. I can honestly say, I know nothing about the cults' plans for any of their diabolical schemes beyond what any other Christian knows who studies God's Word. That is as it should be. The abused person doesn't know the information either. It is locked up in her alters totally inaccessible to her.

The Miry Places and Marshes

But the miry places thereof and the marshes thereof shall not be healed; they shall be given to salt (Ezekiel 47:11).

The miry places and marshes refer to the very root of the sin nature that indwells us. Mire is seen as sin in 2 Peter 2:22, "…the dog is turned to his own vomit again; and the sow that was washed to her wallowing in the mire." The word marshes, (*gebe* in Hebrew), is defined as "reservoir" or "pit." A marsh, in connection with mire (sin) is referring to the place in us where sin is stored, the very pit of sin itself, the very root of the sin nature. This sin nature can never be healed; it can only be destroyed. In previous verses we have seen the sin nature being judged and removed from various aspects of the believer's being. In this verse, the principle of sin itself, as inherited from Adam, is killed.

When any living thing is "given over to salt," it dies. Plants watered with salt water will die, even as fish cannot live in the Dead Sea because of the salt. In Genesis, Lot's wife was turned into a pillar of salt because of disobedience showing us a connection between salt and God's judgment. Here in this Ezekiel passage, we see the final judgment of God upon the sin nature in the believer.

The Hebrew word for "salt," *melach*, means "salt as easily pulverized and dissolved." Jesus is going to pulverize and dissolve the sin nature, the very reservoir of sin, within us. No longer will we have to "reckon ourselves dead to sin" (Romans 6). The very source of all sin, sickness and death will have been eradicated from our being without a trace.

The Pit in SRA

Many survivors will be aware of a place inside called "the pit." It will be found at the bottom of their inner world and is the place where alters consisting of mostly or all sin nature dwell. It is also home to the most powerful demons.

The alters formed during satanic ritual abuse are not haphazardly situated within the survivor's inner world, but instead are intentionally assigned certain places to live. The inner world will have a predetermined structure designed by someone in the cult and placed inside their victim via magic surgery. The child will be shown a small model of the structure which she must memorize before it is "surgically" placed inside. Then as she is tortured, the alters formed are assigned to specific places within the structure.

Torture often begins while the babe is still in its mother's womb. The most common prenatal abuse as evidenced by visions given to the survivors to whom I've ministered, has been needles injected into the uterus. We assume other tortures are possible such as electric shock, dropping heavy objects on the mother's belly or raping the mother.

The fetus can dissociate *in utero*. This is probably determined by a device measuring the baby's heart beat. As torture is administered, the heart rate will accelerate. When it suddenly slows, the baby has dissociated. The cult tries to get as many splits as possible while the child is in the womb. The child's powers will be stronger if the splits are according to satanic power numbers such as 6, 13, or 18. After birth, each split becomes the "seed" to populate a layer in the structure. The following is quoted from my first book *Restoring Survivors of Satanic Ritual Abuse*.

> The alters and furnishings of the inner world are not randomly placed. There is a basic structure into which each person or object is directed. This structure will have as many levels as there were splits in the womb. If a person split thirteen times in her mother's womb, then her inner structure will have 13 levels. There are some instances where the number of splits in utero were not as many as desired, so immediately after birth

the newborn baby was made to split once or twice adding to the number of levels.

These levels or layers should have a geometric shape that often is the same for each level. For example, if squares were used, each level may be a square. Others will have combinations of geometric figures such as squares combined with triangles or circles, for example. Each level is divided into sections or rooms where alters are assigned to live. Demon guards are stationed in strategic places on all the levels. Underneath all these layers will be a pit. Sometimes this pit will have as many levels as the basic structure itself.

The different levels are connected by staircases (often circular) that intersect the gates on each level. It is similar to a high-rise apartment building but the design may be more modernistic because the levels are not necessarily the same size and they may turn at different angles from one another. Often the levels are designed to rotate or spin.

This structure is "placed inside" the child at a very young age. A model of the structure is built and the child is required to thoroughly memorize it. She memorizes the structure including the location of demon guards on each level and the placement of the seed alter on each level. Then through magic surgery the structure is placed inside, and the child is told it will grow with her. During this "surgery" the child believes that she has been cut from her throat down to her lower abdomen and this structure then fills the entire trunk of her body. This becomes her inward reality in a supernatural realm of mind and spirit.

Each alter formed through splits in the womb is assigned to a particular level. This alter on each level becomes the seed which populates through splitting that particular level of the structure. The top level of the structure is called the presenting level. This is where alters that perform the tasks of daily living are housed. They are the ones who clean the house, go to work, take care of the children, communicate with the outside world, etc. These alters are often unaware of each other until it is revealed to them through ministry. They know nothing about the alters on lower levels or that lower levels even exist. Upper level alters were formed by the survivor for the purpose of coping with the challenges of everyday life and are sometimes called the "home system."

The presenting level will most likely have a small number of alters...perhaps as few as seven or eight. The area of this level will be the smallest of all levels. Progressing down through the structure we should expect to find increasingly larger and more densely populated levels. It is common for lower levels to have hundreds of alters. The lower the level the more committed to darkness the alters will probably be.

Cult alters living on the lower levels know all about the upper layers and are able to take control of the entire system. Those alters who are the most powerful and committed to darkness are on the lowest level. When lower level cult alters want to take over the body, they come up through the gates, give a password to each demon guarding the gates, and proceed to the top presenting level. The home system alters have no ability to resist the cult alters and are forced to do whatever they are told. Cult alters may take a home system alter down to a place of torture as punishment for talking or any other infringement. After a time of ministry it may be helpful to pray and ask the Lord to seal the gates so the lower level alters and demons cannot come up to the presenting level and cause trouble. This is not a formula...God has led me to do this with some persons but with others He has instructed me differently. We must be open to the Lord's guidance. (Clark 2010, 131-133).

I believe upper levels of the structure may be in the conscious mind, but the lower levels, more precisely the pit, are in the unconscious, the part of the mind Freud believed was in opposition to the world of order and common sense and was the great corrupter of every day life. He believed that most of us exhibit behavior that works against us and therefore must be coming from another part of our mind we are not aware of. Our conscious mind is not aware of the contents of the unconscious mind, and therefore not able to control it. The unconscious mind, (having, as Freud stated, a life of its own where material develops quickly and more vigorously than material in the conscious mind that is governed by the constraints and reality testing of conscious experience), is the domain of cult alters who work against the person. Freud also said the unconscious mind was the seat of our instincts. This would coincide with what Christians call the sin nature.

Fruitful Trees

And by the river upon the bank thereof, on this side and on that side, shall grow all trees for meat, whose leaf shall not fade, neither shall the fruit thereof be consumed: it shall bring forth new fruit according to his months, because their waters they issued out of the sanctuary: and the fruit thereof shall be for meat, and the leaf thereof for medicine (Ezekiel 47:12).

As I stated previously, a river is often the boundary between countries. This river, Jesus Christ Himself, is the River of Life that touches earth on one side and heaven on the other. In Him both sides of our being, the earthly side and the heavenly side, have come to the same level of holiness. There is no longer the struggle between the carnal side of our nature and the spiritual side because both sides are now pure; carnality is gone, and the fruitfulness of the life of Jesus is seen in the trees. Each tree represents an aspect of the character of Christ, the Tree of Life Himself.

This river is also described in Rev. 22, where we learn these trees are not limited to a short yearly season of fruit bearing but they yield fruits twelve times a year. There is no winter season of death because eternal life has come and the fruitfulness of this life is without end as evidenced by the number twelve. Twelve is the product of the number three multiplied by four. Since three is the number of heavenly completeness and perfection, and four is the earthly number of all that is organic and natural, the multiplication of these numbers will yield unending fruitfulness beyond all comprehension. Heaven and earth have come together in this individual, not just one added to the other, but multiplied, mixed together in a union where one cannot be separated from the other. Twelve is also the number of perfection of government. Jesus now reigns as supreme potentate over every aspect of this believer's life.

These trees are for meat, for doing the will of the Father. This person is now like Jesus when He said, "I have meat to eat that ye know not of," and "My meat is to do the will of him that sent me, and to finish his work" (John 4:32,34). All selfish desires for personal gain and gratification are completely gone from this believer's life and his only desire is to do the will of the Father.

Now "his leaf will not fade," meaning he is no longer subject to sickness, aging and death as seen in Isaiah 64:4 "…we all do fade as a leaf; and our iniquities, like the wind, have taken us away." No longer is there iniquity in his life; therefore, no curse of death is upon him. He has come into the fullness of Christ with a fully redeemed body.

His fruit shall not be consumed because it flows forth from the eternal life of Jesus Christ where there is no end to fruitfulness. In our human frailty, our capability for fruitfulness is limited but here there is no limitation. This person has become a vessel, purified and meet for the Master's use. The fruits of the Spirit—love, joy, peace, long-suffering, gentleness, goodness, faith, meekness, and temperance—flow freely out of him unimpeded by the sin nature. This Hebrew word for "fruit," *periy,* also means "reward." For what greater reward could anyone ask than to feel continually, day after day, perfect love, joy, peace, etc., while walking in complete oneness with Jesus Christ feeling His presence at all times?

Not only is their fruit, *periy,* not consumed, but "it shall bring forth new fruit according to his months." The Hebrew word for new "fruit, " *bikkuwr,* is a different word from the one just examined that meant "reward." This word for "fruit," *bikkuwr,* means "first-fruits" and "new" means "to burst the womb," "to give the birthright." Now that this person has reached the fullness of Christ, he begins to bring in others as the "firstfruits." These people have been in the womb of the church and are now bursting forth to receive their birthright by coming into the fullness of Christ.

This is taking place "according to his months." This word for "months," *chodesh,* means "new moon." The new moon has special significance in Scripture. It is the time for feasting and for blowing of trumpets. (Ps. 81:4) "Blow up the trumpet in the new moon, in the time appointed, on our solemn feast day." The Old Testament purposes for the blowing of trumpets are described in Numbers Ten. They were blown to (1) call the assembly together (2) to announce the time to journey forth (3) to call the people forth to war (4) to celebrate the feasts.

In these last days as God's people begin to come into His fullness, He will call the true Church together. The days of lukewarmness and half-hearted devotion to God will be over. The Church of the last days will be coming together and moving forward on their journey into Christ's fullness. This will be a time of war such as the Church has never known, for all the forces of hell will be coming against the people of God attempting to prevent this great move of His Spirit. Persecution coming from the enemy in an attempt to destroy the Church will only serve to purify it and call the committed forth to new levels of faith, devotion and victory in Christ. This will be a day of feasting on the Word of God as the seals are removed from the Word and new depths of spiritual insight reserved for these last days pour forth from those who have come into His fullness. There will be preaching and teaching such as not heard since Jesus Christ Himself walked on earth. What glory awaits the Church of Christ as it comes into this fruitfulness!

At the same time the trumpets are blowing for the Church, they will be sounding to release God's judgment upon the ungodly. The seven trumpets of Revelation will sound bringing the plagues of God's judgment upon the earth in a dimension such as the world has never seen. In the midst of this great judgment, the firstfruits of Christ, those who have come into His fullness, will be providing by His Spirit, everything needed by the Church because "…the fruit thereof shall be for meat, and the leaf thereof for medicine." When God's people who refuse the mark of the beast can neither buy nor sell, God will provide their food and medicine through those who are ministering from the sanctuary, the place of His fullness and manifested glory. Then will be seen the "greater works" of which Christ spoke in John 14:12. Those who are walking in His fullness, will, in turn, lead others in until Christ will be manifested in His fullness in believers all over the world.

CHAPTER TEN

In the beginning was the Word, and the Word was with God, and the Word was God (John 1:1).

If we want to know Jesus...if we want to draw close to Him...we must start with His Word. It is there we will find a deep and abiding relationship with Him. When we come with thirsting hearts, He will meet us there, and the Holy Spirit, our teacher, will guide us into all truth.

It is impossible to truly know God without delving deeply into His Word. Many Christians read their Bible only occasionally; others read it every day, but few have the habit of daily disciplined study. This is where God wants to take us because He is beginning to remove the seals from His Word. He has many exciting things to show us—many wonderful surprises that could not be revealed until this time—and He is longing for us to uncover them. This is not something reserved only for the Bible scholar with several academic degrees. No! Anyone who is hungry for God and willing to make the sacrifices necessary to search His Word diligently will find exciting revelations that will lift him/her above the flood of last days' judgments into new realms of joy, love and victory in Christ Jesus.

Paul said it was by revelation he went up to Jerusalem (Gal. 2:1, 2). God is calling today's believers up to the spiritual New Jerusalem and we are to ascend "by revelation." The Greek word for "revelation," *apokalupsis*, also means "appearing." By revelation Christ appears to us. Each time we have a new revelation of Him, we see Him a little more clearly. Revelation begets revelation. The more revelation we have, the more we get and I'll warn you of this—revelation is addicting. Once one gets a taste of it, the desire for more leads to deeper longing and more fervent searching.

There are two major prerequisites for revelation that remove the seals from the Scriptures—obedience and sacrifice. Without obedience to the disciplines of prayer and study, revelation will never begin to form in us. This kind of revelation doesn't just plop into our mind out of nowhere but comes through intensive study and a life of obedience. What good is it to study God's Word if one does not appropriate it in one's life? God will only give His precious last days' revelations to those whom He knows are willing to walk in obedience to Him. Notice the word "willing." We cannot always perfectly obey but as long as we are willing and making the effort, God can trust us with His precious revelations.

When we know God's commandments and ways but refuse to obey them, we form calluses on our heart. The more we disobey, the harder our heart becomes making it difficult for us to hear His voice or see His revelations. These calluses, formed through disobedience, are actually veils that separate us from Christ. If we repent and walk obediently, God will begin removing these veils of our flesh so we might draw closer to Him.

Second, deep revelation comes into the life of one who is willing to sacrifice. The amount of time necessary for intensive Bible study requires sacrifice. Others may stay up late watching television or talking while you go to bed early in order to be up before the sun for prayer, study and fellowship with God. Also ministry to others will take time that previously might have been used in pursuit of a favorite hobby or leisure activity. Revelation will flow more freely into a life where ministry flows out to others. If we are not giving out in some way to others, our life can become a smelly, stagnant pond. It is a principle with God, the more we pour out to others, the more He can pour into us.

Revelation flows more freely into the crucified life. If we have not been broken through suffering and if we do not daily take up our cross to follow Jesus (Luke 9:23), we will have little revelation. Great revelation given to an uncrucified life would result in pride and ultimately a great fall. God wants to entrust His greatest secrets to those whom He knows will treasure them in their heart and obediently wait to bring them forth when His Spirit directs. In this way, pearls will not be cast before swine and His Word will not be trampled under foot (Matt. 7:6). Only those who are broken will have the humility and submission to be entrusted with His wonderful revelations.

Many people in their quest for more of God run around from meeting to meeting and conference to conference seeking to experience His presence. Some can only find what they are seeking in worship services where hundreds are attending and worship is exuberant as is often the case at Christian retreats or conferences. Yet God wants us to experience Him every day in the comfort of our own home. He is waiting for us to delve into the Word and partake of the deep well of clear, refreshing water that never runs dry.

As we, the end time church known as the Bride, await the coming of our Bridegroom may we be as Rebekah, who first heard about her future husband by a well (Gen. 24:13). She met a man there, a servant of Isaac, who told her things about him and eventually led her to meet him face to face. She first saw her husband Isaac by another well, the well Lahai-roi where he was awaiting her arrival. Lahai-roi means "that liveth and seeth me." We must believe by faith that when we open our Bible (the well) to study, the Holy Spirit (the Servant) is there to lead us to Jesus (Isaac), and that Jesus is alive and sees us as we come daily to draw fresh water. As we abide in His Word and He abides in us, we will eventually see Him face to face.

Some are like Ishmael and Hagar who only carry water in a bottle (someone else's book or revelation), but bottles eventually run dry and we have to go out and buy another bottle. God has much more for us than bottles. He wants to show us the deep well that is nearby from which we will find an abundant, continual supply of the most delicious water imaginable.

Isaac was not one to depend on someone else's wells; he dug his own. Actually they had been his father's wells that the Philistines had stopped up but he had to dig them again. Others have studied and revealed deep spiritual truths to the Body of Christ, but we come to "own" these truths and carry them in our heart more completely when we too dig deeply and find them for ourselves. In addition to this, we have the added incentive of finding secrets reserved for the Church of the end times.

I live near Lake Ontario. The Great Lakes contain the world's largest supply of fresh water. Buried deep beneath the surface are wrecks of sailing vessels that capsized hundreds of years ago. Many of them carried priceless treasures that still lie hidden waiting for someone to discover. I am fascinated by "*National Geographic*" television documentaries about the recovery of such vessels with their vast historical and monetary treasures. One vessel that has recently been discovered but not yet explored is presumed to be the *Griffin*:

> Ever since the loss of LaSalle's *Griffin* in 1679, the Great Lakes have continued to claim ships. There are literally thousands of shipwrecks littering the shores of the five Great Lakes and tributary waters. What often distinguishes these wrecks from others is their excellent state of preservation. Because the Great Lakes are so cold and because of their relative scarcity of marine life, many wrecks remain intact and undiscovered for hundreds of years. In terms of historical significance, Great Lakes wrecks are unparalleled. [...] it is a startling realization that a short 150 to 200 feet under nearby waters lie many remarkable archeological resources which are largely undiscovered. (Barbi)

I cannot help but see the analogy to the Word of God here. Think of all the wisdom and knowledge and resources for our life that lie just below the surface in our Bibles. All too tragically, many Bibles sit on the nightstand by the bed or on the coffee table gathering dust.

I am convinced many people want to study the Bible but just don't know how. I remember when I felt that way. I would marvel at the wonderful teachings brought forth from the Word by learned teachers and preachers. I hungered for more but when I tried to study, something blocked my way. I think that "something" was just ignorance of the resources available plus my own feelings of inadequacy. I bought some prepared Bible studies at the Christian bookstore, but I found them to be uninteresting. They had you read a Bible verse and answer their question which was either too easy or just confusing. At least, it didn't work for me.

By God's grace I continued to try to study, and over time I "stumbled" into some resources and techniques that worked for me. Study has absolutely transformed my life. The decision to study was one of the most important and rewarding decisions of my life...a decision that will impact all of eternity for me. Hopefully, my decision to study, which led to God's call for me to write, will impact others' lives for eternity too. May God be praised!

Being married to a pastor with master and doctor of ministry degrees certainly helped me in my desire to learn. Although I don't use the study methods he learned in seminary, he was able to open various resources to me. Years ago my husband showed me a concordance and a lexicon and instructed me in how to use them. We also had other Bible resources around our house.

We had a friend, a prophet by the name of Wayne Taylor (who has since gone to be with Jesus), who told me God wanted me to have a book entitled *Types in Genesis* by Andrew Jukes. He had found the book hidden away in some old bookstore, but it was out of print. He had a friend of his type the book by hand! He mailed the manuscript to me. I looked at it a little bit and then put it in a bottom desk drawer where it remained for a few years. During that time, Wayne purchased a scanner and sent me another copy of the book (this time spiral bound) with an attractive cover. I began to read again. This time I continued through to the end. That copy is now dog-eared and underlined with handwritten notes all over the margins.

Others unknown to me realized the value of this old book and began to implore a publisher to publish the book. Kregel Publications came out with a paperback version in 1993. I now have one of these (also dog-eared and written all over) that I mainly use.

Andrew Jukes is not easy to read. His sentences are very long and by the time one reaches the end of a sentence, one may have forgotten the subject. (Sounds a bit like the Apostle Paul, doesn't it?) It is well worth the effort however, because his understanding of allegory unlocks the entire Bible. The keys to understanding all of Scripture are revealed in Genesis in types and shadows. Paul alludes to types when he writes in 1 Corinthians 10:

> *Moreover, brethren, I would not that ye should be ignorant, how that all our fathers were under the cloud, and all passed through the sea; and were all baptized unto Moses in the cloud and in the sea; and did all eat the same spiritual meat; and did all drink the same spiritual drink: for they drank of that spiritual Rock that followed them: and that Rock was Christ (1 Cor. 10:1-4).*

Paul further reveals Old Testament allegory in Galatians:

> *Tell me, ye that desire to be under the law, do ye not hear the law? For it is written, that Abraham had two sons, the one by a bondmaid, the other by a freewoman. But he who was of the bondwoman was born after the flesh; but he of the freewoman was by promise. Which things are an allegory: for these are the two covenants; the one from the mount Sinai, which gendereth to bondage, which is Hagar. For this Hagar is mount Sinai in Arabia, and answereth to Jerusalem which now is, and is in bondage with her children. But Jerusalem which is above is free, which is the mother of us all (Gal. 4:21-26).*

Jesus used allegory in most of his teachings and parables. The Bible is full of allegory throughout the Old and New Testaments. A thorough study of *Types in Genesis*, along with the aid of a concordance and Hebrew and Greek lexicons will help uncover wonderful truths hidden in allegory.

I want to emphasize, though, that true revelation can only come by the Holy Spirit. It is not a function of intellect. When I study I find out everything I possibly can about a topic or a passage. I study it in the concordance and the lexicon, look up the words in an English dictionary, search for the word usage throughout all of Scripture and consult a Bible dictionary. I often still don't know what it means. Then when I have exhausted all my resources, the Holy Spirit will quietly impress the answer upon my mind. I know it is from Him because on my own, I can't figure it out. I have confidence after many years of study, that once I have studied all I possibly can, He is faithful to explain it to me. But first, He wants me to dig for it.

Did you know it pleases God when we study His Word? He really gets excited about it. My abused prophetic friend, who has given me so many prophetic words over the years, once had the following vision for me: She saw the Lord literally dancing around in excitement one time because He saw me sitting in a chair surrounded by stacks of books studying. He had something exciting to show me and He could hardly wait. (Could God really be like that? I think He shows us things on our level so we can understand that He too has emotions and deep feelings about our lives.)

The next morning as I was studying, I had this incredible revelation that led to the writing of this book. I had just completed studying and writing about Ezekiel's healing river. That morning God showed me that satanic ritual abuse is the exact opposite of sanctification...that it was sanctification in reverse. It was then that I started writing this book.

I have included a lot of details here about my entering into study because I want everyone to see that when we have the desire to study and are willing to put forth the effort to try, God will supply all our need. My friend Wayne went to great lengths to make sure I had the book I needed to unlock the allegory of Scripture. My husband showed me how to use a concordance and a lexicon and let me use his until I got my own. God brought me my own personal prophetess to encourage me in my studies. This same woman brought me a book one day entitled *Number in Scripture: Its Supernatural Design and Spiritual Significance* by E. W. Bullinger.

Number in Scripture has been absolutely indispensable in opening my understanding to the verses in Scripture that include numbers. I have done major studies (that will become books some day) that would never have been possible without this book. It was here I learned that when studying for deep spiritual meaning, a number has a spiritual significance apart from its numerical value. For example, in my study of the four living creatures in Ezekiel One, four tells me not necessarily that there were four of them but that they represent human beings in relation to the world and all things created. Bullinger devoted twelve pages of his book to the number "four" alone:

> Four is emphatically the number of creation; of man in his relation to the world as created…Four is the number of the great elements—earth, air, fire and water. Four are the regions of the earth—north, south, east and west. Four are the divisions of the day—morning, noon, evening and midnight. Four are the seasons of the year—spring, summer, fall and winter. Four are the great variations of the lunar phases. (Bullinger 1967, 123)

Bullinger goes on to show how four is used throughout the entire Bible. I have found this book to be absolutely indispensable and never begin my morning studies without it.

When we study in depth, it enables the Lord to take us deep into all areas of our life. Bible study becomes transformational not merely intellectual. When the Holy Spirit brings revelation, it impacts our life. The Lord is most concerned that this time together is relational and life-changing, not just a gathering of information to teach or write about. The flow of revelation is only possible when we are growing and changing with Jesus because we can only see in depth as our heart is able to receive it. Our heart must be right before the Lord in order to see because spiritual truth is perceived through our heart.

When we see deeply beneath the surface of the Word, we begin to see more deeply into situations in our life. We are more perceptive into the lives of those around us. Current events take on spiritual significance as we discern them in light of the Word. Our motives and desires become more in line with Christ's. To study His Word is to feast on the banquet He has prepared and spread before us to strengthen us for the events of the end times.

As we study the Scripture for a greater revelation of Christ, it will be helpful to follow the principles for study outlined below:

Principles for Bible Study

It is most important to approach our study believing the Bible is absolutely perfect in the original languages. Any seeming discrepancies will become our delight because they are usually a clue that leads to a beautiful revelation.

Your study will not necessarily be historical because the historical account is usually the surface account with the deeper spiritual message hidden underneath. Many historical accounts will become very current when studied in this way.

Every word in the passage must be examined in the original Greek or Hebrew using a concordance. I use *The New Strong's Expanded Exhaustive Concordance of the Bible* which includes the best of *Vine's Complete Expository Dictionary of Old and New Testament Words*. It is a mistake to look up only key words because sometimes the seemingly unimportant words provide vital keys for unlocking the passage. Some of the "less important" words are not listed in the above concordance probably due to a problem of space since it contains so much information. If the word I am researching is not in that particular concordance I refer to another Strong's—there are many variations of that concordance.

It is often necessary to use a Greek or Hebrew lexicon for further research into the meaning of a word. I recommend *Thayer's Greek-English Lexicon of the New Testament* and *Gesenius' Hebrew-Chaldee Lexicon to the Old Testament*.

Word derivatives are important. Sometimes just the meaning of the particular word from the passage won't yield any understanding, but looking through all its derivatives will give the necessary insights.

A whole new perspective on an historical passage will appear if the outward account is seen as an inward reality. Those things that happen outwardly in the physical world are only projections of inward reality. Certain individuals may be seen allegorically as inward principles, e.g. ruling mindsets, the human spirit, the natural man, the sin nature, the soul, etc.

Everything in the natural world has a spiritual counterpart. A study of the book, *Types in Genesis,* by Andrew Jukes will reveal many of these. Some examples are: men represent wisdom, intellect and understanding; women are love, the affections and the will; animals are certain emotions; the moon is the church or faith; etc. This book provides many keys for unlocking the most difficult passages of Scripture.

As stated previously, numbers are important for their spiritual meaning rather than their numerical value. *Number in Scripture* by E.W. Bullinger is an excellent resource.

It is helpful to know the meaning of each proper name in a passage. The following are some of the ways to discover these meanings:

A. Look up the word in Strong's Concordance and follow it through all its derivatives.

B. Nearly every proper name in the Bible is listed with its meaning in the Interpreting Dictionary of Scripture Proper Names.

C. If you are studying the name of a place, find out everything that ever happened at that place. This could determine what the place means in terms of this particular passage.

D. If it is the name of a group of people (Syrians, for example), follow their linage back into Genesis and learn from whom they are descended. This can also apply to individuals.

Often there are several Greek or Hebrew words that could be used for a particular English word. For example, there are seven Hebrew words that are translated "company." We need to ask the question, Why did the Holy Spirit choose this particular word? To find our answer we must find the meaning of every Hebrew word for "company" and notice how this particular one differs.

It is often helpful to check where else in the Bible a particular word is used. A computer program such as *Quick Verse* by Parsons is most helpful because you can put in the Strong's number for the word, and it will show you instantly every place in the Bible that word is found. There are several places online such as BlueLetterBible.com where you can find many of these tools.

When studying one small portion of Scripture, we can expect to be studying related passages all through the entire Bible because we are using Scripture to explain Scripture. When we study with this amount of depth, we may spend several weeks on only a few verses.

Look up key words in an English dictionary for an expanded understanding of the word. For example, the number twenty according to Bullinger means "expectancy." *Webster's New World College Dictionary* defines "expect" as "to look for as likely to occur or appear; look forward to; anticipate; expect implies a considerable degree of confidence that a particular event will happen." A synonym for "expect" is "hope."

Remember to record all your findings and store them in well-labeled files for easy access in the future. Without this kind of organization, weeks of studies may be lost that could have been used later to enhance other studies or even a sermon. All studies on your computer need to be backed up on some form of media storage device.

In closing I am adding my findings based on one of my studies about the second coming of Christ that incorporates the principle of "inward" rather than "outward." This one concept alone can open our understanding of many passages regarding the second coming of Christ.

Every Eye Shall See Him

It may be difficult for some to grasp what I want to introduce here because of all the books that have been promulgated concerning the second coming of Christ. People have become famous and made fortunes from bestselling books (some fiction and some nonfiction) that give details of what they perceive will transpire when Christ returns. When people's minds have been trained to think a certain way, it is often difficult to receive a different point of view. I would like to share here some of the revelations God has given me regarding this event. I don't claim to have a full revelation of all the details, but I believe I am seeing some things worthy of consideration.

First of all, is it reasonable to believe God would allow His plans regarding His second coming (something that has been cloaked in mystery since the fall) to be published and read by millions of people? Would He permit movies to be made to accurately portray what He is about to do? I just can't believe that. Our God is a God of surprises. His ways are mysterious and past finding out. Those who looked forward to His first coming were totally caught off guard by the manner in which He actually came. Rather than a rich king born in a palace, they found a humble babe lying in a manger in a stable built for animals. Those who thought they knew the most (Pharisees) had the greatest difficulty receiving Christ or His teachings. Based on the studies I have done over many years, I think we will be very surprised at the way Jesus chooses to reveal Himself at His second coming.

When Jesus returns it will be to establish His kingdom on earth. Jesus said many things directly or in parables about the kingdom of God (or the kingdom of heaven). The kingdom of God possesses the quality of being here in this present hour, and yet it is still coming and is ultimately to come in its fullness. At times Jesus said "the kingdom of God is nigh thee." This Greek word translated "nigh" is *eggizo* meaning "to make near or (refl.) approach." Rather than speaking of a spatial location, He meant it as a spiritual reality…that when we are approaching God, the kingdom is coming nearer to us.

In a sense the Israelites were in the kingdom in Goshen when they experienced God's protection from the plagues that came upon Egypt. Goshen means "approaching or drawing near" (very similar to "nigh" above). We must be approaching or drawing near to Jesus everyday if we are to have His protection when catastrophic events of the end times sweep across our land.

The following scripture, I believe, holds a major key to our accurately understanding at least one important dynamic regarding His coming: "And when he was demanded of the Pharisees, when the kingdom of God should come, he answered them and said, 'The kingdom of God cometh not with observation: neither shall they say, Lo here! or, Lo there! for, behold, the kingdom of God is within you'" (Luke 17:20, 21). Some translators have rendered "within" as "among," but in the Greek, it truly is "within." If we were to examine each passage about the second coming as being about an inward reality, we might find more accuracy than by keeping it outward and physical. We have been on earth learning to become spiritual beings. Why then would the second coming be an outward event not requiring any spirituality? Eventually we will see outward manifestations of the kingdom, but first it must come within us.

Also, there are other passages of scripture that seem to indicate an inward application might be more accurate:

> *And except those days should be shortened, there should no flesh be saved: but for the elect's sake those days shall be shortened. Then if any man shall say unto you, Lo, here is Christ, or there; believe it not. For there shall arise false Christs, and false prophets, and shall show great signs and wonders; insomuch that, if it were possible, they shall deceive the very elect. Behold, I have told you before. Wherefore if they shall say unto you, Behold, he is in the desert; go not forth: behold, he is in the secret chambers; believe it not (Matt.24:22-26).*

I believe we are being warned here that if we are looking for Him to appear in an outward form, we may wind up being deceived. If you see a CNN report claiming that Jesus appears every evening at sunset on a mountain just outside of Los Angeles, don't believe it. If reporters claim Jesus has been seen holding miracle healing services in the desert in Utah, don't go. If your best friend claims to have seen Jesus healing multitudes in a cornfield in Indiana, pray for your friend's deliverance from deception. If you hear that Jesus appeared at the UN and everyone got saved, you can be sure the Antichrist is at work.

Most of us probably would not run to California, Utah, Indiana or New York City to see some purported appearance of Jesus, but what if someone told you He was seen in the sky over El Paso, Texas?...or others had sighted him in the clouds over Houston?...or in the clouds above Jerusalem? Would you get excited? Would you want to go see this phenomenon for yourself? After all, the Bible says He is coming with clouds.

I remember many years ago (pre-Internet) when a photograph of a white robed figure in the clouds (presumably Jesus) was being circulated amongst Christians. Should we believe this as proof that Jesus is starting to appear in clouds? With today's technology, anything that is manifested in the physical realm to be seen with our natural eyes could deceive us. If He is coming with clouds, how can we be sure it is actually Jesus? We might be seeing a hologram projected onto the clouds.

Some passages of scripture reveal that a level of holiness will be necessary in order to see the Lord:

- *Follow peace with all men, and holiness, without which no man shall see the Lord (Heb 12:14).*
- *Blessed are the pure in heart: for they shall see God (Matt 5:8).*
- *Beloved, now are we the sons of God, and it doth not yet appear what we shall be: but we know that, when he shall appear, we shall be like him; for we shall see him as he is. And every man that hath this hope in him purifieth himself, even as he is pure (1 John 3:2,3).*

For many years 1 John 3:2,3 has been one of my favorite passages in the Bible. When we see Christ, we will be like Him! However, in order to be like Him, we have to purify ourselves. We must cooperate with God in becoming pure. It is not something that suddenly happens to us.

If we must be like Christ in purity and holiness in order to see Him, how do we reconcile this with the following verse?

Behold, he cometh with clouds; and every eye shall see him, and they also which pierced him: and all kindreds of the earth shall wail because of him (Rev 1:7).

I have already written about clouds in chapter seven of this book but there is much more to be learned if one takes time to do a thorough study of them throughout Scripture. By way of review...clouds cover over and block our ability to see things. Fog is a good example of this.

Inwardly clouds often represent the veils of our flesh that block our ability to see and experience Christ. When we are obedient to Jesus and willingly deny our self, take up our cross and follow Him, He begins removing these veils.

Also in Scripture clouds are associated with God's glory and presence. He was in the pillar of cloud by day to the Israelites after they left Egypt and in the pillar of fire by night. He was in the cloud over the mercy seat in the Holy of Holies. A cloud descended on Mt. Sinai when God spoke to Moses. The glory of the Lord was manifested in a cloud filling Solomon's temple in 2 Chronicles 5. As we continue our examination of this verse, we will see how our understanding of clouds can expand our revelation.

A casual reading of this verse might cause one to believe that collectively, on a certain day at a specific hour, everyone on earth will look up in the sky and see Jesus in the clouds; but what about blind people? Would they be denied the opportunity to see this most incredible of all experiences? With the earth being round, one side of the earth is in darkness at the same time that the other side is in daylight, so geographically it couldn't happen at one specific hour. It could perhaps be seen worldwide at different intervals in a 24 hour period. However, an inward explanation would be far more plausible. If the kingdom of God is within us, then an inward interpretation would be more likely. Linguistically, "eyes" and "seeing" are words often used to denote understanding. Someone who just mentally grasped what another has been saying might say, "Oh, now I see what you mean."

Here is what I believe this verse is saying: Jesus coming with clouds means He is concealed by clouds; therefore, our vision of Him will not be a full, sudden, complete event but something that occurs gradually. As the veils of our flesh (clouds) are peeled away one layer at a time, our experience of His presence will come gradually. Our hearts and lives must be prepared to receive Him. This preparation requires death to the sin nature (a gradual process) and the relinquishment of our love of the world. As the veils are removed, we will have the realization that we too have pierced Jesus. The process of maturing spiritually involves the realization of how we too have failed to comprehend the preciousness of Jesus. We will know that many times we chose some worldly pursuit instead of time with Jesus and wounded His gentle heart. Things that we thought were acceptable in our life will be revealed to be unacceptable as His light continues to reveal dark places in us. When the clouds are concealing Him, we can't see this about ourselves. As He approaches, His presence enlightens our understanding and we judge ourselves. As we repent, veils are removed and His presence becomes more discernable. *...when he shall appear, we shall be like him; for we shall see him as he is*, and *Blessed are the pure in heart: for they shall see God.*

Seeing Jesus is far more than visual cognition. We truly have no comprehension of His infinite greatness and there are no words to explain what being in His presence encompasses. It will be much more than visual. Every faculty, every atom of our being will experience Him and feel His love. Our human senses—vision, audition, touch, etc.—were designed to perceive and experience our three-dimensional, physical world. Jesus must prepare us mentally, emotionally, spiritually and physically to be able to comprehend His presence. He will lift us up into realms beyond anything humankind has ever experienced.

If we are waiting for Jesus to appear and zap us into perfection, we will be very disappointed. He is calling us to forsake all for Him now. He expects us to spend more time seeking Him than we do watching television, shopping or whatever else we like to do. We must seek Him as though our very lives depended upon Him because they do. Life as we know it is changing quickly. The America we have known is rapidly deteriorating into something far different, and we are going to find that Jesus is all we have to cling to as things we have depended upon begin to crumble. We are going to need to enter into a new realm in God—a supernatural realm of miracles and power, and this will require holiness and sacrifice. Those who are ready and willing to die to the things of this world and go forth with God will find many exciting things waiting to be uncovered. Each new discovery will lead us deeper into relationship with Jesus. The deeper our relationship with Him, the more He reveals to us. The more He reveals to us, the deeper our relationship becomes. It is a wonderful cycle of ever-increasing excitement and joy that makes all the things of this world seem boring by contrast.

Now that we are beginning to see that Jesus wants to reveal Himself to us personally and inwardly, we may be wondering what will happen to the rest of the world that is lost in darkness and sin. The answer is they too will begin to see Jesus, but first they will see Him IN US. The ministry that goes forth from the lives of those in whom the veils have been removed via holiness and to whom the glory of the presence of God has been revealed will stun the world.

There is much yet to be revealed about the second coming of Christ…many things that we do not know…but this one thing we do know—"forgetting those things which are behind, and reaching forth unto those things which are before," we must "press toward the mark for the prize of the high calling of God in Christ Jesus" (Phil. 13b, 14).

WORKS CITED

á Kempis, Thomas. 1952. The Imitation of Christ. Baltimore: Penguin Books Ltd.

Barbi. n.d. Available from www.nightbirdsfountain.blogspot. com/2006/08/great-lakes-shipwreck-griffin.html (accessed 13 September 2006).

Bullinger, E. W. 1967. Number in Scripture. Grand Rapids: Kregel Publications.

Chambers, Oswald. 1935. My Utmost for His Highest. New York: Dodd, Mead & Co.

Clark, Glenn. 2001. "Seeing As Jesus Does." Spirit Led Woman, June/July, 64-67.

Clark, Patricia Baird. 2010. Restoring Survivors of Satanic Ritual Abuse. Five Stones Publishing, a division of The International Localization Network.

Clarke, Adam. 1966. The Adam Clarke Commentary. Available from www.studylight.org/com/acc/view.cgi?book=eze&chapter=047 (accessed 8 November 2006).

Duffield and Van Cleave. 1983. Foundations of Pentecostal Theology. Los Angeles: L.I.F.E. Bible College.

Fonda, M. n.d. Available from www.magma.ca/~mfonda/ freud.html. (accessed 8 June 2006).

Gesenius, H. W. F. 1979. Gesenius' Hebrew-Chaldee Lexicon to the Old Testament. Grand Rapids: Baker Book House Co.

Jukes, Andrew. 1891. The New Man and the Eternal Life. London: Longmans, Green, and Co.

_____. 1993. Types in Genesis. Grand Rapids: Kregel Publications. Originally published 1898. London: Longmans, Green and Co.

Kupelian, David. 2005. The Marketing of Evil. Nashville: Cumberland House Publishing, Inc.

Lawrence and Laubach. 1973. Practicing His Presence. Jacksonville: SeedSowers Publishing.

Nee, Watchman. 1992. The Spiritual Man. Anaheim: Living Stream Ministry.

Nouwen, Henri J. M. 1998. In the Name of Jesus. New York: Crossroad Publishing Co.

Payne, Leanne. 1985. The Healing Presence. Grand Rapids: Baker Book House Co.

Peck, M. Scott. 1983. People of the Lie: The Hope for Healing Human Evil. New York: Simon & Schuster.

www.ingramcontent.com/pod-product-compliance
Lightning Source LLC
Chambersburg PA
CBHW021057090426
42738CB00006B/386